more praise for

The FVN Handbook

"I believe this guide will honor the journey of thousands of people to do the sacred work of reparations and direct action. This path presents a core challenge of not just returning property or resources, but of doing the spiritual work to transform those "items" back into gifts in order to bring forth true reciprocal relationships. And on the direct action side, this path reminds us that so much of what we see, experience and are able to accomplish depends on where we're willing to place our bodies."

Carlos Saavedra
Ayni Institute

"The Fierce Vulnerability Network inspires me in two deep ways. One is the depth of their commitment to align means with ends, which shines from every page of this handbook. The other is their willingness to embrace discomfort and complexity. At a time of deep polarization the world over, their commitment to fierce vulnerability means there is only all of us, without anyone becoming a "them" even while maintaining immense rigor in approaching the tough challenges of our time. I am delighted that after years of careful preparation and deep souls searching, the results are finally available to all who want to do their part in bringing about a livable future. "

Miki Kashtan
author, founder of the Nonviolent Global
Liberation community

"This prophetic experiment in truth offers hope to a society crying out for a better way. Like the testing grounds of Gandhi's ashrams or Black Panther breakfast programs, the Fierce Vulnerability Network is an experiment that promises that rare blend of spiritual sustenance, direct action, and pragmatic problem-solving."

Daniel Hunter
Global Trainings Associate Director, *350.org*

"*The FVN Handbook* is a profound, wise and humble manifestation of the Earth Community's relentless will to creativity and regeneration. It is an exceptionally useful "how-to" guide and how-to fumble towards liberation from every kind of social oppression. Through living into this work and other initiatives, equally bold, broad and specific, we may be able to save enough of ourselves and the living world to secure a future measured in millennia, not decades."

Victor Lee Lewis
transformative social justice educator,
trauma somatics practitioner,
editor of *Lessons from 'The Color of Fear,'*
and Interfaith Chaplain-at-Large

"In this marvelous handbook we glimpse the hearts of creative and compassionate human beings seeking freedom from any number of outworn cultural mandates. I'm speaking of those insidious cultural instructions which tell us to toughen up, to deny our feelings, to hide our vulnerability, to disconnect from our bodies, to deny the truth of our collective reality, to keep secret and lie about our own suffering and failings, and to limit our empathy and compassion to those deemed worthy of it, most often those who look and live as we do. I pray that this very special experiment, this much needed antidote, will flourish. The world longs for just such beautiful and tangible examples of love, vulnerability, generosity and healthy service."

Rev. Lynice Pinkard
Black writer, pastor, public intellectual,
and movement chaplain;
author of the prophetic essay
"Revolutionary Suicide: Risking Everything
to Transform Society and Live Fully"

NOMADIC PRESS

OAKLAND

PHILADELPHIA

XALAPA

WWW.NOMADICPRESS.ORG

MASTHEAD
Founding Publisher
J. K. Fowler

ASSOCIATE EDITOR
Michaela Mullin

DESIGN
Jevohn Tyler Newsome

MISSON STATEMENT Through publications, events, and active community participation, Nomadic Press collectively weaves together platforms for intentionally marginalized voices to take their rightful place within the world of the written and spoken word. Through our limited means, we are simply attempting to help right the centuries' old violence and silencing that should never have occurred in the first place and build alliances and community partnerships with others who share a collective vision for a future far better than today.

INVITATIONS Nomadic Press wholeheartedly accepts invitations to read your work during our open reading period every year. To learn more or to extend an invitation, please visit: www.nomadicpress.org/invitations

DISTRIBUTION
Orders by teachers, libraries, trade bookstores, or wholesalers:

Nomadic Press Distribution
orders@nomadicpress.org
(510) 500-5162

Small Press Distribution
spd@spdbooks.org
(510) 524-1668 / (800) 869-7553

This book was made possible by a loving community of chosen family and friends, old and new.

For author questions or to book a reading at your bookstore, university/school, or alternative establishment, please send an email to info@nomadicpress.org.

Cover and interior art by Rachel Rolseth
Cover collage and concept designed by Jevohn Tyler Newsome

Published by Nomadic Press, 111 Fairmount Avenue, Oakland, California 94611

First printing, 2022

Library of Congress Cataloging-in-Publication Data

Title: ***The FVN Handbook***
p. cm.
Summary: We are the *Fierce Vulnerability Network*, a constellation of direct action teams positioned at the intersection of racial healing and climate justice. Fueled by fierce vulnerability, the power of emergence, and the promptings of our own vocations, we practice reparations and take direct action together. If you're seeking healing, belonging, and creative life-affirming ways to engage, crack open this handbook! You may have just found your spiritual home base within the movement.

[1. REFERENCE / Personal & Practical Guides. 2. EDUCATION / Collaborative & Team Teaching. 3. EDUCATION / Organizations & Institutions. 4. EDUCATION / Philosophy, Theory & Social Aspects. 5. NATURE / Environmental Conservation & Protection] I. III. Title.

LIBRARY OF CONGRESS CONTROL NUMBER: 2022935492

ISBN: 978-1-955239-29-5

THE FVN HANDBOOK

The principles and practices of the
Fierce Vulnerability Network

THE FVN HANDBOOK

The principles and practices of the Fierce Vulnerability Network

NOMADIC PRESS

Welcome

Deeply aware of the humbling enormity of the crises humanity is facing and our own imperfections, we are nonetheless determined to act. As we move forward, we pledge to listen, learn, experiment, and grow; to make our mistakes, adapt, and try, try again.

We are one element in an expansive movement ecosystem, a "movement of movements," each part of which is essential. Within this movement ecosystem, our network is called to two inseparable core commitments:

1 **To contribute to racial healing & reconciliation** by making and facilitating concrete acts of reparations.

2 **To honor, uplift, and defend life** through bold civil disobedience and creative initiative to address racial injustice and the climate emergency.

We are assembling direct action teams of courageous people who feel called and are prepared to uphold the network principles and practices (aka "the DNA") outlined in this handbook.

We long to see what life wants to do through us. We resist the temptation, therefore, to predict or to attempt to shape the outcomes of this experiment by way of fine-tuned mission or vision statements.

We simply hold trust that the teams we assemble—if true to the DNA described in these pages—will offer beautiful and sacred gifts to the continuing struggle for justice and wholeness.

Contents

Foreword by brontë velez — i

Introduction Origins of the Fierce Vulnerability Network — vii

Important Note to the Reader: FVN's Soft Launch — xiv

The Defining Marks of Our Network — xvi

Foundation

Toward Collective Liberation — 1

    Patriarchy: a central blueprint of domination — 4

    Where we draw our wisdom and guidance — 6

    The inseparability of racial justice and climate justice — 8

    Fostering real diversity and inclusion — 11

An Integral Approach Geared Toward Direct Action — 13

A Home Within the Wider Movement — 17

Core Commitments

Network Core Practices — 23

    Reparations — 25

        Atonement = at—one—ment — 26

        Balancing the systemic and the personal — 30

        Relationship / Racism and its impacts — 31
            are not "one size fits all"

Reparations take three deeply intertwined 32

    forms within our network

Positionality 34

Core Practice: reparations self-audit, dialog 36

    and action

Recommended practices 39

Direct Action / What is direct action **42**

and where does it happen?

Our commitment to strategic planning and action 43

One-off actions and strategic initiative 45

Two ways of taking strategic initiative 48

Taking action at the intersection of climate and 50

    racial justice

Emotional release, protest and direct action 53

Is a "riot" strategic? 54

Where are the "frontlines"? 56

The intersection of direct action and disaster 57

    relief/mutual aid

Relationship with police 59

Considerations for arrest 62

Core Practice: 21 days of direct action 63

Fierce Vulnerability **67**

Fierce vulnerability and the human nervous system 70

More on trauma and trauma healing 72

Fierce vulnerability and integral nonviolence 74

A nonviolence foundation   78

The field   81

Relationship to security culture   84

Core Practice: quarterly reflection circles   86

Recommended practices   88

Recommended practices for tending to the field   92

Vocation   **93**

Roles vs. vocations   95

Recommended practices   97

Emergence   **101**

Coming back to earth   103

Decentralized and self-organizing   104

Recommended practices   105

Network Structure

Basic Structure, Membership, and Onboarding   **110**

The Wider Movement Ecosystem   **111**

Network Communities   **113**

Members / Teams   **114**

Forming a team   116

Pollinators and pollinator teams   118

Team size   119

Leaving/dissolving a team   120

Key reflection questions and tips for teams   123

Collectives   **125**

     An aspirational national collective structure   127

Nationwide Localism / How To Join   **129**

     the Network

The Onboarding Process Still Being   **130**

     Developed

Our Living Systems

Principles of Self-Organizing   **134**

Five Operational Systems   **135**

Decision-making: how we determine   **137**

     a way forward

     Needs, principles, and tools   138

     Sample agenda   139

     Three basic meeting roles for teams and collectives   142

     Tech-free meeting spaces   143

     Advice process   144

Resource flow: how we deal with money   **147**

     Practicing relational economics   149

     Internal and external reparations / Where money   151

     lives and how it moves

     Sharing costs for events   152

     Empire tax resistance   156

Information flow: how we communicate   **158**

     Technology and information flow   159

On the matter of encryption / Determining your   160

   team's information flow protocol

Feedback loops: how we learn from each other   **166**

Types of feedback   167

Feedback process   168

Giving feedback   170

Receiving feedback   174

Differing feedback cultures   176

Restorative conflict engagement: how we fight   **178**

and make up

Trauma and conflict   179

Restorative conflict engagement processes   181

In the case of a serious breach of network DNA   186

Dismissal from the network   187

The essential role of trust and connection   188

Appendices

Core Network Practices / Reparations self-audit   **193**

   Direct action resources / Points of intervention   **199**

     Spectrum of allies   201

     198 methods of nonviolent direct action   202

     Action agreements   208

   Quarterly team reflection circle   **210**

An Aspirational Vision of a National Structure   **213**

   Core Collectives   **214**

Power and Access Collective (partially centralized)

Onboarding Collective (centralized)   218

Coaching Collective (centralized)   220

Conflict Engagement Collective   225

(partially centralized)

Network Feedback Collective (centralized)   229

Internal Reparations Collective (not centralized)   232

DNA Revision Collective (centralized)   233

Stewardship Circle (centralized)   235

Decision-Making and Meeting   **236**

Format Resources

Resource Flow and Cost-Sharing for Events   **240**

Principles of Gift Economics   **241**

Five Economies for Breaking Free   **244**

from Colonial Capitalism

Community Welcome Statement   **248**

Principles of Environmental Justice   **249**

Rupa Marya on Colonization   **252**

Five Opportunities for Healing and Making   **254**

Room for Growth

For Starting/Grounding Meetings   **255**

and Gatherings

Additional Resources

Climate Crisis   258

The Inseparability of Racial Justice and   259

    Climate Justice / Reparations and Atonement

Direct Action   261

Fierce Vulnerability and Integral Nonviolence   262

Emergence   264

Decision-Making and Information Flow / Resource Flow   265

Feedback and Conflict Engagement   266

Self-Organizing/Decentralization   267

Contact   269

Acknowledgments   271

Foreword

When i think about forewords, i think about what and who precedes us. i think about reverence, libations, offerings to ancestors, well-trodden paths, seeds and memory. i think about the black feminist ethic and impulse toward citation; the wisdom and protocol that an elder speaks before a youth.

following in that lineage, i preface my offering with Chicana lesbian activist Cherríe Moraga's admonition in "This Bridge Called My Back," that:

> "...we need political memory, so that
> we are not always imagining ourselves
> the ever-inventors of our revolution;
> so that we are humbled by the valiant
> efforts of our foremothers' and so with
> humility and a firm foothold in history,
> we can enter upon an informed and re-en-
> visioned strategy for social/political
> change in decades ahead."

the authors and practitioners of the wisdom in this text are deeply informed by a political memory that adheres to a lineage of nonviolence and direct action as significant tactics to instigate change. and they also embody the audacity to permit that lineage to evolve and meet the epoch we are in; especially, as we navigate nurturing livability and abolition in the midst of climate collapse and late-stage capitalism.

the co-conspirators of the Fierce Vulnerability Network describe this as a "handbook," but as i dove deeper into the text it read more like an almanac. it made me think about how important it is that knowing the weather allows us to anticipate what we need to be equipped with in order to be protected in that weather. and here, i'm thinking about weather, as in Dr. Shawn Ginwright's language of "persistent-traumatic stress environments," and weather, as in Christina Sharpe's, "the Weather as the totality of Black peoples' environments."

as a descendant of enslaved black folks, i think about how the Weather is unbearably humid—not a sacred, detoxing humidity: the kind of sweat that shakes the demons off—but an oppressive climate, sticky with the remnants of un-commemorated hauntings, or on the other end, crowded with the dissociative celebration and memorialization of hauntings. as someone who grew up in the shadow of Thennthlokfee (Muscogee) turned "Stone Mountain," the largest confederate monument in the U.S., i have lived my whole life in that weather.

it's a humidity that snatches the breath up from underneath you—from police brutality to polluted cities to raging wildfires birthed from colonial fire suppression to the prison-industrial complex to coronavirus; the weather of our times takes our breath away. and if this is the weather, then this text signals: what are we being asked to put on and take off to meet this moment?

Bayo Akomolafe's theology and scholarship at the Emergence Network invites us to consider, "What if the way we respond to the crisis is a part of the crisis?" and to that point, i believe so much of the way we are responding to the crises of our times reinforces these crises because the dominant origin stories for how we arrived to this moment are riddled with erasures.

if the story is that we arrived to this epoch deemed the "Anthropocene" through humans-at-large industrializing and extracting from the planet, then our response methods for transforming the Anthropocene might look a lot like how folks are responding right now: continuing the myth that humans are not useful to this planet and that the earth would be better off without us, the idea that we can do business-as-usual and make capitalism more sustainable, the idea that we can save the planet through our individual consumer choices or technology, or even better that the wealthy can corrupt the earth and then leave it behind for outer space.

or, we could re-historicize this epoch we are in, try on words like the plantationocene (Donna Haraway, Anna Tsing), which positions the inauguration of this epoch through the forces of colonialism, enslavement, white supremacy, indigenous displacement and genocide, and cisheteropatriarchy. to hold that these violences were so distinct, so geological in fact, that they changed the weather of our planet.

when we wade through the spiritual and ancestral implications of climate collapse and re-frame their origins in this way, the questions to guide our methodologies towards repair shift—we may instead begin to ask:

1. what are our respective inheritances
    across difference?

2. what does our liberation have to do with
    one another's liberation and the more-than-
    human world's liberation?

3. what has yet to be commemorated?

4. what are the hauntings that live between us
    and in the places we inhabit?

5. what do relational and ritual reparations look like between communities that are descendants of enslavement/indigenous genocide/displacement and descendants of enslavers and colonizers that accrued wealth through that harm?

6. what does the egregious lack of atonement have to do with the weather of this moment?

these are the questions this book responds to. this text is a forecast that we cannot move forward in our freedom work without the intersections of racial and climate justice being woven together. it is a prophetic methodology for liberatory organizing where how we get free is not just a destination but a practice we embody through revelatory kinship. it is a prayer that reparations follow a path of "commemorative justice" (Free Egunfemi)—that reconciliation is not "charity" but a relational commitment to atonement. that harm that has been caused will not be remedied through just moving money but rather will require ancestral inheritances (financially, socially and spiritually) to radically transform.

and this text has the audacity to call you in to join in changing the weather, from wherever your gifts align with that transformation. there is a prayer here for an ecological belonging where we each hold something sacred to offer to this planet and to one another. it is a hospitable text that is relevant for anyone seeking a critical and comprehensive organizing framework for movement practices committed to not only liberation as an end but as a means.

the crafters of this handbook offer careful provocations for how we hold space with one another through tenderness, how we can work through conflict with grace, how we defend what we love

through integral nonviolence and "direct action as ceremony," how
we love one another and this planet with fierce vulnerability. all of
these practices are deeply beneficial whether or not you formally join
the "network." these friends describe their organizing frameworks as
"DNA" and it's my belief this material seeks to be a fugitive encoding
that equips us with the power to transform harm at a molecular
level; where network slips through the boundaries of formalities and
instead becomes a mycelial spirit of liberation that can't be stopped,
spreading like good fire, like alchemy.

i pray you enjoy ~

brontë velez
co-founder and creative director,
lead to life

Introduction

The Origins of the Fierce Vulnerability Network

Our story begins in the fall of 2015, when three friends started talking with each other about forming a network of small teams to respond in diverse ways to the climate emergency. In the context of white supremacy in the US, they also saw the need to put reparations at the center of this vision, along with a commitment to integral nonviolence (a threefold practice of self-healing and transformation, community uplift, and nonviolent direct action to protect life). They were deeply influenced by Mahatma Gandhi and his founding of ashrams where those deeply committed to integral nonviolence lived, practiced, and took action together.

After a few initial conversations among themselves, these three men sought reflections and advice from an informal women's wisdom council and from trusted elders. After integrating feedback from these friends, and receiving their blessing to move forward, the plan developed to host an in-person gathering in April 2016 for two weeks at the Possibility Alliance, a nonviolence-based electricity-free, fossil fuel-free intentional community in La Plata, Missouri.

The Missouri gathering was named the Movement of Movements (MOM) gathering, in honor of the diverse movement ecosystem we wanted to be of service to. We realized all along that what we were building would be just a small part of the larger macro movement ecosystem. Fifty-plus people attended the MOM gathering, including representatives from Be The Change Project; Operation Nonviolent Life; DIRI; GRUB (Growing Resourcefully Uniting Bellies); Loving Earth Sanctuary; Beyond Extreme Energy; Vine and Fig (New Community Project); Living Downstream; Living Energy Farm; Joyfield Farm; Christian Peacemaker Teams; Casa de Paz; Taos Initiative for Life Together; Community Rights Groundwork; Evening Star Farm; Carnival de Resistance; Sing Alive; and more. Beloved elder, Laurence Cole, supported and nurtured the group with song-leading and grief-tending.

The MOM gathering ended with teams deploying to St. Louis, to join a group of Diné (Navajo) and Hopi activists from Black Mesa, Arizona, and members of the local Black community who staged a direct action at the headquarters of Peabody Energy. The action brought awareness to the corporation's contamination of the land, water, and air of Indigenous peoples, and included a call for reparations. This became a tradition for the next few years—whenever the network met, we aimed to participate in a direct action led by BIPOC communities under assault. We also collected resources to distribute to BIPOC groups. We wanted our theory of change to be grounded in practice.

Just after attending the MOM gathering, in April 2016, Jimmy Betts (at the time working as a lead organizer for Beyond Extreme Energy) got involved in the water protector camps at Standing Rock on the lands of the Dakota Oyate. He nudged others from the MOM gathering to get involved in the struggle to stop the Dakota Access Pipeline. Over the next year, dozens of MOM participants joined in actions at Standing Rock as well as resistance to the pipeline in Iowa. Involvement in this movement had a deep impact on the emerging vision for the network.

The next gathering, composed of six activists/organizers, took place and was hosted again by the Possibility Alliance, in spring 2017. It lasted one month and included a decolonization workshop with anti-racism trainer, Elaine Enns, at Saint Isidore Catholic Worker Farm and a mutual aid trip to Little Creek Camp, an Indigenous-led camp resisting the Dakota Access Pipeline in Iowa. Those assembled for this gathering were the first to see themselves as a "DNA-building team." The Momentum model of organizing defines DNA as an organization's *story, strategy, and structure.* Over time, our DNA-building teams used the phrase *principles and practices* interchangeably with this Momentum framework. The first iteration of the network's five core pillars came out of this Spring 2017 gathering: defense of life (direct action); reparations and atonement; integral nonviolence; activating people's vocation; and emergence (as illustrated by adrienne maree brown in her book *Emergent Strategy*).

In January and February of 2018, a new and more formal group of DNA builders convened for a gathering hosted by Vine & Fig and Living Downstream in Harrisonburg, Virginia, for three and a half weeks. One week of the gathering was dedicated to planning an action under the leadership of the Lumbee Nation and Black farmers affected by the Atlantic Coast Pipeline. After a multi-day deep listening tour and planning period, the group occupied the Governor's office in Raleigh, North Carolina, for eight hours before being arrested. Along with many of the groups listed above, new groups that participated in this gathering were the Climate Disobedience Center; Cultural Catalyst Network; Indigenous Iowa; The Indian Problem; Jerusalem Farm; Tap Root Sanctuary; the Poor People's Campaign; and the Cascade Project.

At Evening Star Farm, in Viroqua, Wisconsin, in the summer of 2018, the third DNA-building gathering occurred. The network teamed up with the Poor People's Campaign on two actions—one risking arrest to bring awareness to the lead contamination in drinking water for the Black community in Milwaukee, the other taking over an empty Wisconsin Senate room at the capitol in Madison and running a people's senate, interspersed with movement songs reverberating throughout the capitol building. This gathering marked the launch of the network's zine which summarized the network's DNA up to that point. The gathering also featured a deeply impactful and enlightening coaching session with Carlos Saavedra, co-founder of Momentum. Three hours with Carlos took the DNA-building team's understanding of self-organizing to a new level.

Circulation of the zine spurred growing interest, and people began to refer to the network as YTBN, the Yet-to-Be-Named Network. A new DNA-building configuration, composed of a mix of DNA builders from the Harrisonburg and Viroqua gatherings, decided it was time to host another larger gathering to experiment with an initial onboarding process for prospective network members. This gathering was held at Green Valley Farm in Sebastopol, California, in the second week of December 2018. More than 50 people attended, including children. Together this group participated in what ended up being something of an onboarding rehearsal, rather than an official onboarding process. The reason for this was that over the course of the gathering's first few days it became apparent that the DNA wasn't complete enough to provide a robust container for official network members and teams.

The Sebastopol gathering featured many presenters, including guests from Movement Generation, Nonviolent Global Liberation, Coming to the Table, and the Mechoopda tribe of the Maidu people. Lynice Pinkard's article "Revolutionary Suicide— Risking Everything to Transform Society and Live Fully" was one of the core guiding documents for the weekend, and Rev. Pinkard's stirring oratory was a profound highlight for many. Our time together also included a grief ceremony, presentations from local Black and Indigenous community leaders, and a musical performance by the duo MaMuse, composers of the network's informal theme song, "We Shall Be Known." The gathering put into practice the network's emerging reparations commitments, with thousands of dollars being moved to several BIPOC organizations in the Bay Area. New organizations represented at this gathering (along with many of those listed above) were Canticle Farm, East Point Peace Academy, and Weaving Earth. At the end of the week, those gathered selected a new group of people to become the network's DNA-building team and gave them the mandate to complete the DNA and continue the launch of the network.

The new DNA-building team had three week-long gatherings in the spring and summer of 2019, in Boulder, Colorado; Oakland, California; and Madison, Wisconsin. Through these meetings the material that you find in this handbook took shape, building on the YTBN zine and overall framework developed by previous DNA-building teams. The group did further experimentation in reparations work together and spent time deepening their relationships and hosting events introducing local people to the network. During the Oakland gathering, a day-long coaching session with Miki Kashtan, founder of Nonviolent Global Liberation, proved invaluable, especially with regards to the network's organizational systems.

That same summer, members of the DNA-building team and trainers from East Point Peace Academy led a Fierce Vulnerability weekend for 150 participants at the annual gathering of the Fellowship of Reconciliation chapters of Oregon and western Washington. This training represented a pilot of a weekend workshop that the DNA builders envisioned as core content for what they hoped (and still hope) would eventually become the network's onboarding process.

In the fall of 2019, three additional weekend Fierce Vulnerability trainings were led by members of the DNA-building team with support from East Point Peace Academy trainers. These took place in Boulder, Colorado (in Oct); Madison, Wisconsin (in Nov.); and in Oakland, CA (in Dec). At that time, with a first draft of this handbook complete, the DNA-building team coming out of Sebastopol dissolved and named a final "home stretch" DNA-building team. This "home stretch" team was charged with settling a handful of remaining DNA matters, including differentiating between the network's core practices and recommended practices, determining what the network's decision-making system would be, and what shape the national structure would take. This team developed new content related to fostering diversity and inclusion as well.

In 2019 and 2020, groups around the country began experimenting with forming teams based on the DNA in this handbook. Unsurprisingly, these "teams-in-formation" were dramatically impacted by the COVID-19 pandemic. Planned trainings were moved online and local teams-in-formation had to reevaluate and adjust their work together. During this time the network was not able to host the in-person gatherings that had been so critical to the network's birthing journey for its first three years. Nonetheless, local teams-in-formation participated in protests and actions in the wake of George Floyd's murder and were also very involved in the Indigenous-led struggle against the Line 3 pipeline in Minnesota.

There are many other examples of actions taken by teams-in-formation during this period, spanning several regions of the US. Bay Area teams-in-formation were deeply involved in a 40-day Reparations Procession in the Bay Area, during which participants walked 9 miles every day, inspiring the redistribution of over $90,000 to BIPOC groups in the Bay area. The Harrisonburg and Belfast teams-in-formation deployed to support resistance to the Mountain Valley Pipeline (MVP) with Appalachians Against Pipelines (featuring a giant 12' mama wood duck and her many ducklings). Teams-in-formation in New England led and participated in the "No Coal No Gas" Campaign in New England, blocking coal trains and hauling coal out of the Merrimack Generating Station in New Hampshire, the last coal-fired power plant remaining in the region. The Ventura County group organized to stop a southern

California methane compressor from being rebuilt across the street from an elementary school in Ventura, California.

In the spring of 2021, existing teams-in-formation met monthly from January to April to compare notes about their experiments and experiences with the network's DNA so far and to learn from each other. Groups represented in these calls were: Boulder, Colorado; Madison, Wisconsin; Harrisonburg, Virginia; Northern Vermont; Western Massachusetts; New Hampshire; Ithaca, New York; Omaha, Nebraska; Belfast, Maine: Ventura County, CA; and Oakland, CA.

In the fall of 2021, catalyzed by the opportunity to publish our handbook with Oakland-based independent publisher, Nomadic Press, YTBN decided on a name for the network, based on many discussions and ideas. Ultimately, the wider network community chose *Fierce Vulnerability Network*, which we believe captures the spirit of this unique experiment.

We have been working with this DNA for five years now and have enough direct experience to feel good about publishing what we have learned together. At various points in the creation of this handbook, members of the DNA-building teams played a major role as "managing editors" of the document, working to form and compile the content that eventually became the book you hold in your hands. As of this writing in early 2022, members of the Sebastopol and home stretch DNA-building teams have reconvened to meet monthly to support the launch of this handbook and the activists and organizers we hope will be supported by it.

Despite all that's gone into its creation, *The FVN Handbook: The Principles and Practices of the Fierce Vulnerability Network* is only a seed, a beginning. We hope you will take this handbook and plant it in your communities, organizations, movements, imaginations, and hearts, and that you'll actively, lovingly tend what grows there.

Important Note to the Reader

FVN's Soft Launch

This first edition of *The FVN Handbook* describes the guiding principles, shared practices, and organizational systems that bind our network together. It is important for you to know, however, that the handbook does not yet include a description of the onboarding process we hope will soon offer people a pathway to official FVN membership.

Until such an onboarding process is in place, we are inviting all those who have carefully reviewed the DNA set forth in this handbook, and who feel called to live it out in practice, to organize themselves into teams, on an unofficial basis. Just as the unofficial teams up until now have played such an instrumental role in shaping the network's DNA, we hope and expect that the experimentation of a new wave of unofficial teams will yield invaluable learning which will inform our future onboarding process.

You will also notice that while this first edition of the handbook offers many ideas and a general sense of direction about an overarching national structure for the network, it does not include a clearly defined map of one. As with the evolution of our onboarding process, we fully expect that the experiments and feedback of our unofficial teams will greatly inform the design and implementation of our future national (and potentially international) structure.

Essentially, the document in your hands is an invitation to you to help FVN in its ever-evolving process of becoming. Trusting in the strength of our relationships and following the principles of self-organizing, we will come back together at a time when we have learned what we need to learn, and developed what we need to develop—at which point we will update *The FVN Handbook*. We very much hope you will be part of this creative, living process.

As the content of this handbook was crafted, it was largely framed in aspirational language which not only describes the network at the time of this writing, but also the network to be. Because of this,

> until we have an official onboarding process in place,[1] please keep in mind that all references to members and teams in the handbook should be translated by the reader as unofficial members and unofficial teams.

In a world where we are taught to have all the answers in place before embarking on a big undertaking, where the work plan is supposed to be set, and the timeline agreed upon, it's a bit unnerving to publish what remains a work in progress. At the same time, it's exciting to do so, and we experience it as a sincere expression of our commitment to emergence. We'll explore that commitment in detail in the coming pages. For now, suffice to say that, like Dr. Martin Luther King Jr, we're learning that, "Faith is taking the first step even when you don't see the whole staircase."

Come what may, we lovingly welcome you to this beautiful experiment.

---

1. Visit thefvn.org to stay updated on the status of our development of the onboarding process and national structure for the network.

The Defining Marks of Our Network

Foundation

We long for **collective liberation**, for healing of people and planet. We long to be of service to life.

We are guided by the spirits of our ancestors and the wisdom of the natural world, of which we are a part. We believe this to be **sacred work**.

Our work is guided by our shared understanding that **racial and climate justice are inseparable**.

We are a direct action network rooted in **an integral nonviolence approach**. In addition to direct action, our work encompasses self-transformation and community uplift (the work of building sustainable, regenerative and just communities).

We seek to be **a grounding, communal, spiritual movement home** for one another, from which a fuller expression of our gifts and ourselves can be brought into the wider movement ecosystem.

Core Commitments

We hold two core commitments that are
the primary "what" of the network:

1. Making **reparations** real; and...

2. **Direct action** at the intersection of
   climate justice and racial justice.

We hold three additional commitments that
represent our primary "how":

3. Embodying **fierce vulnerability**;

4. Discerning and lifting up **vocation**; and

5. Responding to and placing our trust in
   emergence.

Core Practices:

While each team in the network determines the unique ways in
which they embody the network's DNA, all teams share three core
practices in common:

1. Completing and following through on
   the **Reparations Self-Audit, Team
   Discernment Process and Action Plan**

2. **Engaging as a team in a minimum of 21 days per year of direct action** at the intersection of climate and racial justice.

3. **Quarterly team reflection circles** to support individual and collective learning, connection, and conflict engagement.

Network Structure

We are a mostly **decentralized** network **with some centralized elements**. We follow principles of **self-organizing**.

Our network is composed of **members** who are organized into **teams** of 3–8ish people. Teams provide members a home of mutual belonging, support and accountability and serve as the main home base for engaging in the network's core practices.

When members discover that something important is missing in the network, or that something beautiful can be added, they are encouraged to form **network collectives** to meet those needs and opportunities. Teams and collectives exist within a supportive **network community**, which in turn exists within the expansive context of relationships, communities, campaigns, and movements that make up the **wider movement ecosystem**.

To support equity and efficiency, and to create organizational coherence across the breadth of the network, our teams and collectives align our organizational systems with our purpose and values. We aim to make our **decision-making**, **resource flow**, **information flow**, **feedback**, and **conflict engagement** systems explicit, voluntary, nonviolent, and reflective of our core commitments.

Our network does not have a budget and we are not staffed. While several organizations have dedicated staff time to support the launch of the network during its early stages, **the network has no vision of becoming an organization**.

Key Yet-To-Be-Developed Components of FVN Structure

As discussed in the previous note about our network's "soft launch," at the time of this writing we do not yet have an official **onboarding** process in place, nor do we have a clear overarching map of our network's **national structure**. To learn more about the status of these key elements, see the Network Structure section.

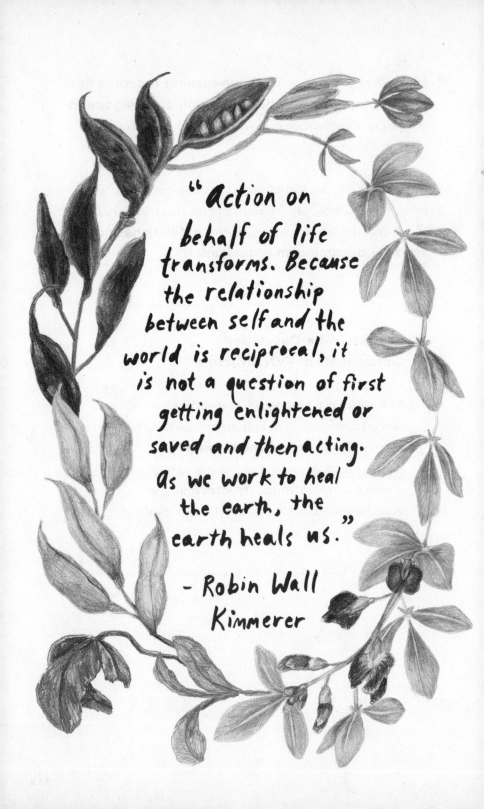

"Action on behalf of life transforms. Because the relationship between self and the world is reciprocal, it is not a question of first getting enlightened or saved and then acting. As we work to heal the earth, the earth heals us."

- Robin Wall Kimmerer

FOUNDATION

Toward Collective Liberation

"When culture is based on a dominator model, not
only will it be violent, but it will frame all
relationships as power struggles."
~ bell hooks ~

We recognize that our network's core direct action and racial healing commitments express themselves within the confines of an overarching system of domination—one that extends in a multitude of overlapping directions: patriarchy, racism, capitalism, obsessive resource hoarding, the ownership and exploitation of human bodies, the devastation of war and militarism, and the colonization of nature.

The domination system turns human beings against one another, against the land, and against our own deeply held natural intuition to thrive together.

Our earthborn instinct compels us toward liberation. We strive, therefore, to overcome systems of **separation** and **domination**, and to build and nurture communities of **belonging**. We aim for this through practices rooted in soulfulness, camaraderie, connection to the natural elements, and in the emotional tenderness of recognizing our need to be seen and held in community. We experience connection, personal healing and transformation to be essential to our pursuit of collective liberation. We long for these to be at the heart of what we do.

Here are some of the ways we move in this direction:

- When we **recognize the interdependence** of all life and acknowledge **the dignity and humanity** of all people and species, we are combating the worldview of separation.

- When we remember that **reparations is healing** and that **direct action can be ceremony**, we remind ourselves that **this work is sacred**.

- When we position ourselves in a place of **love and curiosity** we are unlearning oppressive indoctrination.

- When we restore ourselves to **an embodied connection with the natural world**, we come in touch with aspects of ourselves that domination would rather see erased.

- When we **embrace our whole selves**, are **fiercely vulnerable** with one another, and **take action together**, we directly resist a culture that says we are powerless.

- When we resist **consumerism and winner-loser capitalism** and **reconnect with abundance**, we get a clearer glimpse of reality.

- When we **interrupt "power-over" dynamics** in our personal interactions and group processes we are disrupting white supremacy and patterns of patriarchy.

We openly acknowledge that whatever attempts we make to repair centuries of damage will only represent a wildly incomplete work in progress.

We are nevertheless called to do something now to address the legacy of colonization—genocide, slavery, theft, kidnapping, and so many other forms of brutality and dehumanization—knowing we have nothing near an adequate solution. We expect our methods and understanding to change as we move forward, and we will continue to turn to the leadership of those most impacted as our network evolves.[2]

We do not know what will turn the tide on climate or bring racial justice and healing to the billions who yearn for it. As we pursue collective liberation we know that cultural norms around "effectiveness" and "efficiency" can make us value winning above all else. This view of "winning" creates an end result that requires someone to "lose." Our commitment to collective liberation challenges us to move beyond this winner-loser binary. We do not, therefore, see our network as an "organization" attached to particular "results."

> **We are not here to win** and we are not here to tell other groups how they should do their work. We are here to be our true selves and to **serve life.**

---

2. See the Appendices for a potent illustration of the impacts and dynamics of colonization, by Rupa Marya, a medical doctor who has devoted her career to fighting racism in the medical system.

Patriarchy: a central blueprint of domination[3]

We're painfully aware that our communities struggle with overlapping sources and forms of oppression.

We name patriarchal oppression here at the beginning of this handbook because it so insidiously enters into movements fighting for justice, and because we believe there can be no pathway toward genuine racial healing or climate justice that does not include bold resistance to patriarchy.

At its root, **patriarchy** has served as one of the central blueprints of domination in human society, and it lives on as a deeply ingrained worldview. Passed on from generation to generation, this system of beliefs and actions perpetuates separation and power over others.

Patriarchy preys upon every human across the spectra of gender and sexuality. But if we liken patriarchy to a weapon, sexism, cisgenderism, misogyny, and heteronormativity are the **tip of that weapon**. The impacts of gender violence are both seen and unseen. They are severe and far-reaching, showing up in innumerable forms of subjugation, disrespect, and disregard of women, queer, trans, and non-binary people.

We practice undoing this system in many ways, such as honoring our emotional selves, embracing humility and releasing the urge to control, valuing each other in ways that subvert gender

---

3 . For the purposes of our handbook, the word patriarchy serves as a wide umbrella encompassing two other important variations, heteropatriarchy and cisheteropatriarchy. Throughout the handbook we've struggled to balance our desire for precision with our language with our desire that the language remain as accessible as possible to a broad spectrum of folks drawn to the network. We know there's a cost in either direction. We hope the overall content does well enough to fill in the gaps.

constructs, and educating ourselves and engaging in deep personal inquiry about the ways patriarchy is playing out in each of us.

> "The underlying principle of patriarchy is separation and control. The separation is from self, other, life, and nature. The fundamental structures we have created over these millennia are based on dominance and submission, and the worldview we have inherited justifies them as necessary to overcome both our basic nature and "Nature", seen as separate from us."
> ~ Miki Kashtan ~

In our network DNA we have resisted treating patriarchy as an isolated silo or bucket. It's too pervasive for that to be enough. The work of undoing patriarchy, therefore, punctuates this entire handbook, deeply informing our core practices, recommended practices, organizational systems, and—imperfect and messily human as it is—our shared culture.

Where we draw our wisdom and guidance

We view our network as one small link in a chain that goes back countless generations, bringing forward the **wisdom of our ancestors.** This chain also moves many generations ahead, nurturing the **life and energy of our yet-to-be-born descendents.**

We know that **we are not alone**, and we are not so arrogant as to think that we can catapult a transformation of our society by ourselves.

So we sit. We slow down. We listen. Our guidance does not come only from books about political resistance or academic papers about racial justice. We listen to the depths of our hearts. We seek connection with the spirits of our ancestors. We listen for our deepest, truest desires, from where the wishes of future generations emerge.

> "Another world is not only possible, she is on her way. On a quiet day, I can hear her breathing."
> ~ Arundhati Roy ~

This listening is not only for the voices of our human relatives. The story of life on earth did not start with us. Our story did not start with humans, as the homo genus to which our species belongs evolved out of millions of years of struggle, learning, and growth by other species.

The houseplant on your desk, the hummingbird drinking nectar from the flower outside your home, the hawk gliding through the sky, the majestic blue whale the size of your house—**all are our relatives**, in a real and tangible way.

The delusion of separation from, and a sense of superiority over the more-than-human world is at the heart of much of the destruction caused by our species. We may see ourselves as the most "evolved." Yet watching the murmuration of thousands of starlings, the multigenerational flight patterns of monarch butterflies, or the communication between trees in the forests made possible by mycelium networks reminds us of the deep wisdom that these beings offer us.

Late stage capitalism and our modern society can drown out the subtle ways that these messages are transmitted. But we know that we are not going to be able to think our way out of the challenges of our times. We are not going to use our intellect, alone, to "solve it."

Many of the practices of our network—silence, candlelight, singing—are ancestral practices that supported our ancestors in listening. We are in need of that same support now, and so we gratefully follow their example.

The inseparability of racial justice and climate justice

Another essential touchstone for us in our pursuit of collective liberation is the understanding that climate justice and racial justice are utterly intertwined.

The ransacking of the human and more-than-human world, which drives climate change and all of its devastating consequences, has been and continues to be fueled by colonialism and the violent, systemic oppression of **Black, Indigenous, and People of Color (BIPOC).**[4] In the US context, racial injustices such as police terror, mass incarceration, the disappearances and murders of Indigenous women, mass deportation, and detention camps in the borderlands run hand in hand with the many ways that BIPOC communities are hit first and worst by both the impacts and causes of climate change.

Among other factors, including grossly racialized wealth deficits and underinsurance, BIPOC communities are far more likely to face extreme challenges in recovering from climate disasters such as superstorms and wildfires, the resulting displacement, as

---

4. We're using the term BIPOC (Black, Indigenous, and People of Color) as an acknowledgement that Black and Indigenous people experience particular forms of injustice and systemic racism in the U.S. context that can be obscured by the use of "People of Color." We considered PGM (People of the Global Majority) because it subverts the dominant narrative in our society that people of color means "minority," which carries the connotation of less than, and which is grossly inaccurate in a world where white people are by far the minority. In the end, we chose BIPOC because in the final months of drafting the handbook, this formulation has become increasingly widespread and has been more widely adopted by the individuals and groups it references. We understand that none of these terms are perfect, and they can create as many questions as they resolve. We also know that language evolves over time, and at this current time, we feel that this term best meets our needs.

> "You can't have climate change without
> sacrifice zones, and you can't have
> sacrifice zones without disposable
> people, and you can't have disposable
> people without racism."
> ~ Hop Hopkins ~

well as pandemics like COVID-19 that arise from the disruption of ecological systems. Compared to white people, BIPOC communities have significantly higher exposure rates to air pollution, landfills, lead poisoning, water contamination, and hazardous waste sites. The fossil fuel industry is notoriously racist in determining where to extract, refine, transport, and dump its spoils. The industrial food system preys on low-income BIPOC communities. The compromised health of BIPOC communities due to all these factors exacerbates a vicious death-dealing cycle.

The current crisis requires a social response unlike any seen before—an all-hands-on-deck response of massive proportions. For that to be possible, our network believes that relationships created, sustained, and transformed by trust and honesty are absolutely essential.

Our network's commitments to reparations and to taking direct action for racial justice are, therefore, completely interwoven with our commitment to climate action. Without reparations and direct action against white supremacy, we don't see how we can make our way to the racial reconciliation and healing we long for, and which we believe are prerequisites for the level and quality of mobilization the climate emergency requires of us.

We acknowledge that the contemporary climate movement was born out of the environmental justice movement, which grew out of the organizing of visionary BIPOC leaders in impacted communities. The ignoring and erasure of this history is a painful casualty of white supremacy. For a powerful glimpse into that history and its deep relevance to our current situation, see the "Principles of Environmental Justice," drafted and adopted by the delegates to the First National People of Color Environmental Leadership Summit, October 24-27, 1991, in the Appendices.

Fostering real diversity and inclusion

Transparency about our network's racial makeup so far

Our network's origins can be traced to collaboration between a couple dozen activist-organizers, the large majority of us white, who shared a deep commitment to making reparations and climate justice real in our lives and communities.

From the beginning, a small number of BIPOC people were instrumental in shaping this process, a few as members of our core group, and a larger circle offering deeply impactful feedback. It's critical to acknowledge, however—especially in view of the fact that racial healing is at the heart of our network's DNA—that the predominant whiteness of our group set significant limits on how the beginning stages of our work were envisioned and carried through.

A crucial both/and

We know from our own experience and from observing the efforts of many others that having a heartfelt desire and intention to bring together a multiracial, multicultural community is not enough. In our white supremacist society, the gravitational pull toward white normativity is so strong that unless structures are put into place to deliberately counteract it, many spaces can become and remain white dominant.

Our network draws inspiration from groups that have taken systemic steps to counteract this pull toward whiteness, in order to create spaces that are racially representative of their communities. Our commitment to fostering diversity moves us to do the same.

But fostering diversity is just one step in the critical process of becoming the network we long to be. Having more people in the network that represent the communities we're living and working in is critical, but genuine inclusion means building a culture that gives everyone a lived experience of belonging and shaping the work.

Our network is committed to racial healing and to racial and climate justice. If we're going to make a genuine contribution in these areas we need to ask ourselves some serious questions, and let our answer to those questions result in action.

```
What are the missing perspectives tied
to our core aims?
```

```
What systems, education, training,
trauma healing, and ways of being will
nurture a network culture of equity and
belonging?
```

Mirroring the previous network statement on patriarchy, our commitment to fostering diversity and inclusion extends well beyond race. Diversity and inclusion across a great breadth of experience and identities—race, gender and gender expression, sexuality, class, legal status, history with the criminal justice system, education, religion and spirituality, vocation, and more—makes our network more robust, addresses crucial areas of undeveloped awareness, and leads us further into integrity.

An Integral Approach Geared Toward Direct Action

This threefold combination has guided and strengthened change-makers and their movements across the globe, across history:

```
                    Direct action,


          Community uplift, and


Self-transformation.⁵
```

Collective direct action is central to our coming together as a network. We are deeply and actively engaged in other crucial work as well, in our lives and in our communities. Deep work of self-transformation and hands-on engagement in the society-healing work of community uplift are essential features of the network. These types of work overlap and complement one another in many powerful ways. The iceberg model on the following page helps illustrate the mutually supportive nature of these interconnections.

---

5 . Mahatma Gandhi originally described these pieces of work as "self purification," "constructive program," and "satyagraha." For a more complete discussion of these concepts, see Chris Moore-Backman's *The Gandhian Iceberg: A Nonviolence Manifesto for the Age of Great Turning,* Be the Change Project, 2016. The Momentum Community's Movement Ecology training and the Buddhist Peace Fellowship's Block/Build/Be program also provide further resources.

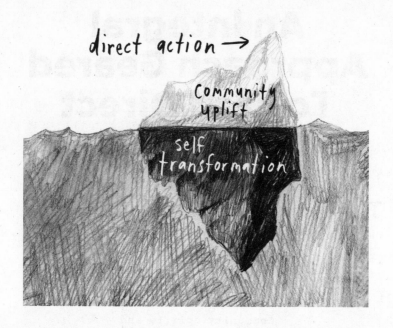

Self-transformation. The biggest, weightiest part of the iceberg—the enormous underwater mass—represents the work of aligning our personal choices and behaviors with our deepest principles. If we do not dismantle our own internalized patriarchy, racism and colonization, and heal through the resulting trauma, we are likely to reproduce it or be complacent to patterns of it in our work. If we do not openly challenge how our own behaviors and worldviews contribute to the destruction of the biosphere, we will likely replace one form of environmental exploitation with another. If we don't treat each other differently, we're going to repeat and multiply harm.

This, of course, is the story of trauma repeating itself across generations. Simply put: hurt people hurt people. While the work of self-transformation is often the least outwardly visible, we hold it to be utterly essential and foundational. For many in our network, it is fueled by spiritual practices and connection to what we hold as sacred. This aspect of nonviolence does not develop only out of good

> "Building community is to the collective as
> spiritual practice is to the individual."
> ~ Grace Lee Boggs ~

intentions or through ideology; it requires significant practical and intentional work.

Community uplift is where our commitment to align principle and practice moves from the personal realm into the wider community. This is the work of building a new, nonviolent society within the shell of the existing, exploitative, and destructive one.

This includes a great variety of culture-shifting, economic, ecological, educational, religious/spiritual, relational and direct service initiatives. Regenerative agriculture, forming new approaches to group process and decision-making, responding to harm in ways that center healing, sharing resources to reduce our ecolog-

> We believe it is essential that **direct action** is carried forward in tandem with the **work of self-transformation** and the **creation of meaningful alternatives** to the systems we are working to dismantle.

ical impacts, how we treat our elderly and educate our youth—any form of building life-supporting structures to replace the existing extractive systems are all examples of community uplift.

Each member of the network engages in their own combination of such initiatives, and we've built in many throughout the network, including **making reparations real**.

Direct action, the outermost tip of the iceberg, means directly intervening in violent systems and situations to immediately stop harm. It is where our inner transformations, our courage and creativity, our grief, rage, and fierce love move us into choice-full confrontation with systems and forces of domination.

This is where our **private heartbreak** becomes our **public witness** and our unseen power is released. When we stand in front of 10,000 tons of coal traveling by train, or between militarized police and a targeted community, when we defy laws to see the homeless housed and the undocumented protected, we are telling the truth about the world around us in powerfully disobedient ways—challenging the assumption that "that's just the way things are." Direct action is our deliberate engagement in constructive conflict, putting our bodies into action to clear the way for the fullest expression of our humanity and for the building up of the nonviolent society we long to inhabit.

```
Our best guess is that the full-blown soci-
etal change we long for cannot come into
being unless each piece of this threefold
approach is being practiced powerfully in
the world. Our lived experience also leads
us to believe that each component needs the
other two in order to be fully activated.
```

A Home Within the Wider Movement

From the beginning our network has seen itself as a small ingredient within a complex and magnificent recipe. We are not in this to show others the "right" way to do things, or to convince others to join us in what we're doing—unless, of course, it's a genuinely snug fit. We're in this because we want to bring our particular offering into the greater mix of what is sometimes referred to as the "movement of movements." We are inspired and grateful to learn from others, to share what we've learned, and to keep learning together within the broader movement ecosystem.

This network isn't for everyone. Those who become members of the network do so because this particular community, and the particular principles and practices that bind us together create a unique home for us within the larger movement ecosystem.

Many of us have experienced deep feelings of alienation in movement settings because of the mix of convictions and longing we hold: the inseparability of racial and climate justice, the interconnection of personal, social and systemic transformation, and the importance of not dehumanizing others—very much including our "opponents." We long to bring both halves of "fierce vulnerability" into the work, a bold and embodied commitment to justice, and an openness and heart-centeredness that make connection and healing possible.

For many of us, our love for the indescribable beauty of this earth, our deep knowing that we are not separate from it, and our most sincere desire to listen to the callings of earth itself have led us here.

Reversing generations of racial violence and climate disaster is a **BIG project**, and we won't be able to do much of anything if we are acting alone as isolated teams, or even as an isolated network. The many activist groups, coalitions, faith communities, organizations, and campaigns that make up the movement ecosystem are essential to this undertaking. We are all in this struggle and opportunity together.

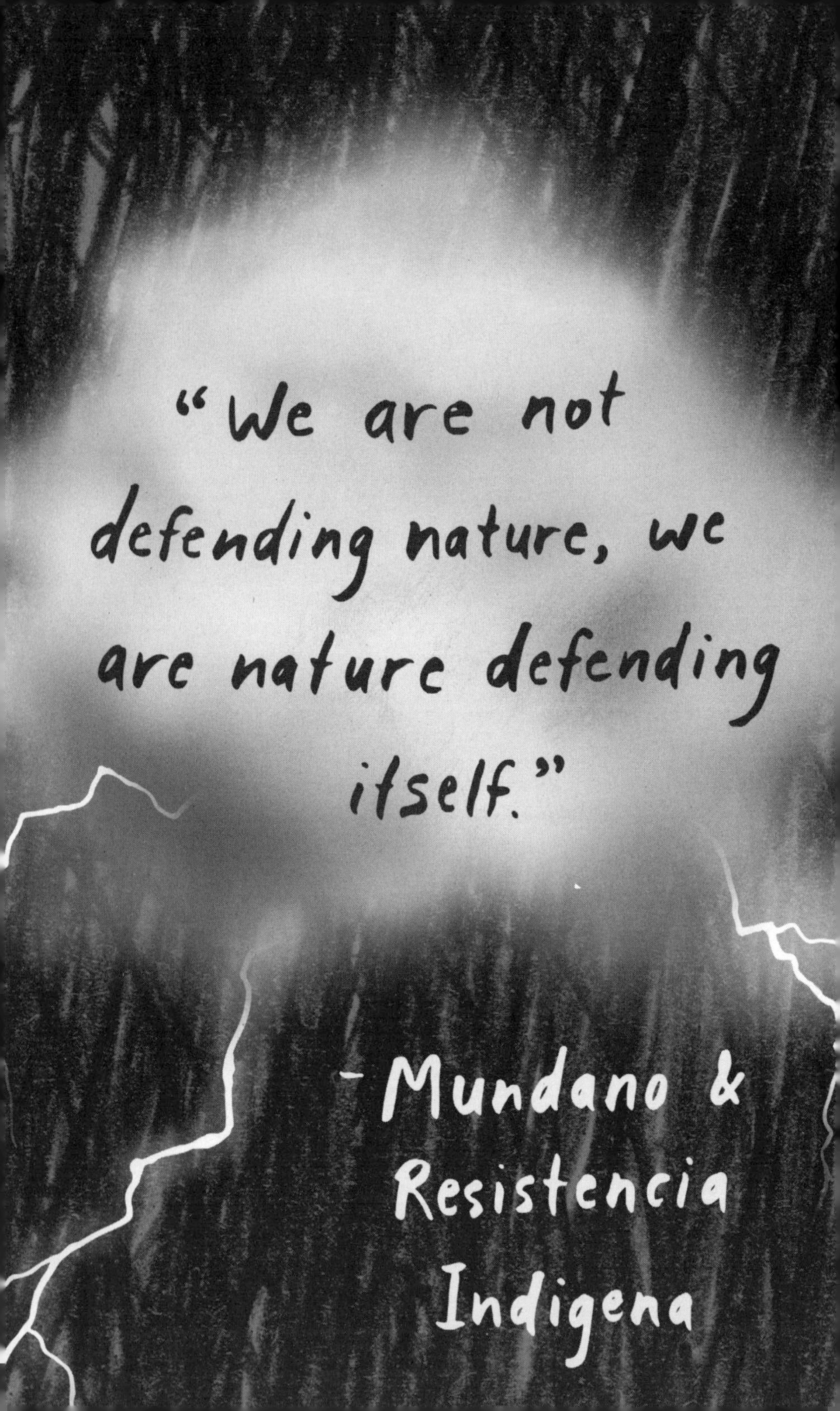
"We are not defending nature, we are nature defending itself."
-Mundano & Resistencia Indigena

CORE COMMITMENTS

Network Core Practices

Our network holds five core commitments: reparations, direct action, fierce vulnerability, vocation, and emergence—each of which is covered in more detail in this section of our handbook.

Because we want these commitments to make a tangible difference in our lives and communities, all members and teams in the network also commit to the following network-wide **core practices**:

1. Completing and following through on the network's commitment to reparations, which includes: completing a self-audit and team discernment process, then creating and following through on a team action plan. See the Reparations section for more.

2. Engaging as a team in a minimum of 21 days per year of direct action at the intersection of climate and racial justice. See the Direct Action section for more.

3. Gathering quarterly as a team for reflection circles to support individual and collective learning, connection, and conflict engagement. See the Fierce Vulnerability section for more.

In addition to our network's three core practices, we strongly encourage teams to also experiment with a variety of recommended practices corresponding to each of the five core commitments.

We encourage each team to choose practices that resonate deeply, experiment with them, and determine together if you want to continue that practice or drop it. These recommended practices, which you will find listed at the end of the sections to follow, are designed to deepen your team's embodiment of the network's DNA and to strengthen your relationships with one another. In addition to the three core practices, the recommended practices will also serve as a guide for how to spend time with your teammates.

Reparations

Returning, not giving.
Reparations, not charity.

Racial healing in our society requires tangible expressions of reparations.

Reparations must be at both the systemic and personal levels.

Restitution for past harm must be combined with direct, impassioned struggle for racial justice here and now.

Attempts to repair centuries of damage done represent a wildly incomplete work in progress.

Atonement = at—one—ment

To understand our network's reparations commitment is to understand our take on the word atonement. In short, for us, **both reparations and atonement begin with an acknowledgement that a wrong needs to be rectified. This wrong is rooted in the mistaken belief that we are separate from one another.** Wisdom traditions the world over describe this as a fundamental human delusion which sets the stage for human domination in all its forms—from racism to sexism to the subjugation of the more-than-human world, and on and on.

We understand atonement to be **a collaborative, ongoing process of the heart and mind, leading to actions that bring healing and connection.** Constructing the society we long for demands courage and audacious action. **We will all make mistakes.** And as we move forward, we will be called upon to risk making bigger mistakes beyond the rules of "woke culture." We commit to turning to face each other as we learn from these mistakes. Curiosity will be our guide in healing and growth. Building and repairing, we will strengthen our communal fabric.

In our experience, atonement actions fall into two broad categories:

1. **Relational work to change the way power manifests itself in and beyond our teams.** This work supports healing—both personally and interpersonally—and opens the possibility for healthy interracial relationships within our multiracial network. For white people this is often referred to as the work of "being an ally"

or "being an accomplice." For those who have been marginalized historically, this is the work of reclamation, empowerment, and self-determination. We see reparations as a deeply significant material component affecting both sides of the coin in this transformational process.

In the US context, "the wrong that needs to be rectified" has been most clearly named by Black and Indigenous people, who for centuries have called for reparative restitution for the unspeakable crimes of white people against them. Particularly, we acknowledge that the movement for reparations has come largely from Black communities. We want to acknowledge this history and the hard work that brought this movement to where it is today. We also acknowledge that our network's commitment to reparations is broader than the Black-white analysis that sometimes permeates conversations about race. While Black people and white people have a very particular history and lineage that needs to be healed, we also know that for any of us to receive true healing, relationships between ALL communities must be healed.

2. In order to do this relational work, there is the internal work of awakening that people with privilege—especially white people—need to do to repair their broken lens. This work helps people see the distortions that whiteness creates in our world and enables them to repair at least some portion of the damage this distortion has caused. This is often referred to as white people "doing their work."

Simultaneously, there is the internal work that BIPOC people need to do to recover from the historical and ongoing trauma of racism and colonization. This is the work of revitalization, re-membering, and reconstruction of identity and communal relations.

We commit to this work while acknowledging that most of the damage that's been done can never be undone. We now set out to move in the direction of creating the social relationships that ought to have existed from our beginnings. As such, atonement and reparations are inextricably linked. Our starting point is the owning of our past, from which we move to repair a small portion of the incalculable damage that's been done, and in doing so, to contribute to the building up of the society we long for. **This work of atonement and reparations flows from love, kinship, and responsibility.**

Are you and your team aware of or involved with campaigns fighting for systemic victories inclusive of the five following United Nations' defining marks of reparations:

1. CESSATION, ASSURANCES AND GUARANTEES OF NON-REPETITION. To ensure whichever crime against humanity these reparations address has ceased.

2. RESTITUTION AND REPATRIATION. What our network refers to as "returning what can still be returned, repairing what can still be repaired."

3. COMPENSATION. Because so much cannot be repaired or returned.

4. SATISFACTION. To address moral damage, such as "emotional injury, mental suffering, and injury to reputation." When cessation, restitution, and compensation do not bring full repair, further satisfaction is often needed. An example of this could be formal public apology.

5. REHABILITATION. Care and services (such as legal, medical, and psychological) to be provided for those impacted by the oppression.

Balancing the systemic and the personal

Reparations must be both systemic and personal. The possibility of full-fledged reconciliation depends on full-fledged redistribution. Any sincere redress for unspeakable crimes against humanity requires action on a societal scale that individuals can never accomplish in isolation. While keeping this big picture imperative in view, our network also sees the importance of individuals reckoning with their own unique connection to the call for reparations. We therefore ask all our members to find meaningful ways to make reparations real at the personal level.

The network encourages its individual members and its teams to determine for themselves the balance they want to strike between personal and systemic reparations work. The network's Reparations Self-Audit process (discussed below) is designed to support this process.

Related to the systemic side of the reparations equation, we gratefully acknowledge the Movement for Black Lives (M4BL) Reparations Toolkit, which highlights longer-term reparations campaigns that have brought about far-reaching, holistic reparations gains. **We encourage our members and teams to make time to research whether reparations campaigns are currently underway, in or beyond their communities, toward which they feel called to lend their organizing and activist energies—including, when invited and appropriate, taking direct action. We also encourage teams to explore the question of whether or not they may want to initiate longer-term, holistic reparations campaigns themselves.**

Relationship

Relationships are key throughout the process of practicing reparations. We also acknowledge that while many white people are often desperate for connection and healing across racial lines, those who have been on the receiving end of oppression are best suited to set the pace for such trust and relationship-building, if they so choose.

White members of our network commit to these practices without expecting anything in return, including relationships, and without attempting to dictate the pace of any relationships that do begin to take shape.

These practices have been (and will continue to be) shaped by a process of feedback from people from very differing positionalities.

Racism and its impacts are not "one size fits all"

The Movement for Black Lives bears witness to the pervasive anti-Blackness that gives rise to very specific and horrifying patterns of police brutality, criminalization, hate crimes, and bigotry. The Missing and Murdered Indigenous Women movement bears witness to the terrifying reality that Indigenous women are murdered at a rate ten times higher than other ethnicities. The Close the Camps movement bears witness to the fact that our society reserves particular forms of punishment and dehumanization for undocumented people from Central and South America.

In our effort to contribute to racial healing through reparations, it's vital to remember that white supremacy—while destructive to every human being—doesn't fall on us equally, and that there are deeply painful fault lines within the BIPOC community.

The traumatic impacts of racism and white supremacy don't fall on racial groups equally either, and one of the most important things our network's reparations redistribution can support is the trauma healing[6] of the people who need it most. This can take many forms, such as intensive ongoing work with an experienced trauma healing practitioner or program.

And at times, depending on the circumstances, it might look like something much simpler. Maybe a needed source of healing energy will come in the form of an afternoon off work or spent in nature. Or maybe it's an hour of empathic listening and support from a friend. Maybe it's a one-off massage, or a delicious, healthy meal prepared and delivered with love.

The point is that people from marginalized communities face enormous hurdles day in and day out. **Our network cultivates and celebrates a reparations practice that welcomes opportunities, both large and small, to support their wellness.**

Reparations take three deeply intertwined forms within our network

For too long, longstanding calls for reparations have gone unanswered. Our network now moves to heed them, believing that doing so opens up the possibility of profound personal and interpersonal healing. We also believe that doing so is a precondition for racial

---

6 . For more on trauma, see the Fierce Vulnerability section, the Conflict Engagement section, and *Five Opportunities for Healing and Making Room for Growth* by Resmaa Menakem in the Appendices.

reconciliation. To the extent that this level of societal healing is achieved, the possibility opens up for a truly transformative movement to emerge.

We take actions in making reparations using a three-part framework originating from the work of Rev. Lennox Yearwood Jr., President and Founder of Hip Hop Caucus:

1. **Financial** (land repatriation/rematriation, and wealth redistribution): We need to move the land and money. It's about time.

2. **Physical** (direct action under the leadership of impacted communities): Contribute sweat equity and risk, including putting one's body in the way of injustice and in support of frontline communities.[7]

3. **Spiritual**: (atonement and trauma healing): We cannot merely manipulate systems of economy and repatriate/rematriate land. Reparations cannot simply be something that happens within the context of the capitalist system, which is at the heart of so much of the harm we are trying to undo.

---

7. For a description of frontline communities, see the Direct Action section.

Many of us must make spiritual amends to one another for complicity, for history, for the things outside our control for which we are nonetheless accountable. We must tend to the deep wounds that white supremacy has inflicted on all of us, including ancestral healing of intergenerational trauma and the reclamation of our connection to land and to each other.

Positionality

Black, brown, white, immigrant, Asian or Pacific Islander, and Indigenous people make up this network, and often more than one of these identities is held by a single individual. This means we are all in a different relationship to the land we walk upon and to the impacts of white supremacy. Additionally, there is a huge difference between wealth and income, as there is between generational poverty and situational poverty (the latter of which is generally caused by a sudden crisis or loss and is often temporary).

Acknowledging the complexity of our differing/ mixed/intersecting racial identities and financial situations, all members in our network are committed to making reparations real. **We expect that the vast majority of network members who will be returning stolen goods will be white-identifying people, and that those in the network who identify as BIPOC will most often either receive reparations, help create appropriate justice-serving pathways for their team's redistribution, and/or play an instrumental role in whatever repara-tions organizing or campaign work the team might choose to take up.** For example: one Black member of the network created a scholarship fund for BIPOC youth to have access to leadership development opportunities, and participates in making reparations real by encouraging others in the network to direct reparations to that project.

While white poverty is very real and deeply unjust, the network's reparations practice is not a platform to address it, and we are careful not to conflate classism with racism. For this reason, all white-identifying people in the network are expected to offer some form of reparations. For those truly without money[8] this could look like fundraising for others, offering time and labor, or sharing and redistributing non-financial resources.

On a closely related note, because the violence of poverty is inflicted on so many people in our communities—including white people—we understand that our movement ecosystems must include mutual aid for people of all races and backgrounds—for example, by supporting one another through illness, financial hardship, debt, and disaster.

Obviously, the racial makeup of each team will shape their reparations process in significant ways. We suspect a certain quality of emergence will inform conversations as teams navigate consent, relationships, and positionality.

We encourage BIPOC team members on multiracial teams to speak their needs in team discussions about reparations, including access to self-care resources.

---

8. Things are relative and everyone's story and circumstances are unique. It is also the case that many people with hundreds of thousands or even millions of dollars think they can only spare a few hundred or a few thousand dollars, even though if they were without any money tomorrow, they would still have many other resources, including family support, ability to work, and safety nets of various kinds. People who have experienced poverty are often more likely to share their "last dollar" with others. We seek to engage in courageous self-inquiry and courageous conversation with one another about how much is enough, and how much is best understood as surplus.

We suggest that teams with white members identify a goal for team-generated reparations based on the shared results of the team's self-audit processes. Teams may choose to organize a communal pool or to return resources separately (see more below). In any case, the network commitment to making reparations real requires that teammates name their commitments to one another and support one another to follow through.

Teams made up of all BIPOC members may choose to help direct and facilitate the flow of reparations commitments from the wider network community, and/or to advise teams in the network who would like to get plugged into pre-existing reparations projects or campaigns or who have an interest in launching a reparations project or campaign of some kind themselves.

Teams made up of all white members should be extra careful to study, listen, and learn from this handbook and other resources, as well as from multiracial and BIPOC teams in the network, wherever such opportunities are offered.

Core Practice: reparations self-audit, dialog and action

Our network's first core practice takes place in three steps:

Step 1: Reparations Self-Audit

Each team member completes a Reparations Self-Audit, which includes exploration of personal lineage, ancestry, relationship to resources and extraction, details about one's financial situation and relationship to money, familiarity with reparations history, and knowledge about current reparations initiatives in or beyond their locale. All of this will be explored in order to determine the nature of each member's participation in their team's reparations commitment (to be determined collectively by the team in Step 3).

For people who identify as white, this will most likely include a commitment to the redistribution of money and potentially land for repatriation/rematriation.[9] BIPOC teammates may include a request that reparations flow to them, or to other BIPOC-led movements and projects that they suggest. See the Appendices for the full self-audit.

Step 2: A real conversation about money and resources

Each team will gather, with members sharing the experience, stories and outcomes from their self-audit. This sharing will include what each member discerns about their individual commitments. Teams may choose to gather with elements of ceremony and candlelight to honor the tender nature of this sharing.

These conversations about reparations are meant to lead us into a space of radical financial transparency, of leaning into discomfort and away from the conditioning that it's not okay to talk about money. This moves us more fully toward our purpose of finding a

---

9. While the network clearly encourages teams to practice and foster the practice of repatriating/rematriating land to its original Indigenous stewards, it also encourages and celebrates the redistribution of land to Black people. While Black communities may not have an ancient ancestral tie to the land, the legacy of their forced and violent displacement from their own land, and their centuries-long stewardship and cultivation of land in the U.S. is claim enough. Teams may also choose to redistribute or support the redistribution of land to other BIPOC groups, such as disenfranchised Latinx farmworkers whose labor has fed the US since the 19th century.

movement home and changing the systems of the world that do not honor life—one of those being the money system.

Step 3: Make it real and track it

Create a team action plan that incorporates all team members' individual reparations commitments, and potentially additional collective reparations commitments. This action plan should include, if applicable, commitments to explore, continue, or deepen

```
Consider the scale of impact: How might
donating $100 to a non-profit compare to
paying for a $100 train ticket for someone
traveling to a network event or moving $100
to a local Indigenous land trust? Consider
what such differences might mean for you
and your team.
```

involvement with pre-existing reparations projects or campaigns at a systemic/institutional level, and/or any action steps that may have emerged regarding the potential launch of any new reparations project(s) or campaign(s). Remember: The who, what, where and how of practicing reparations enables us to make this commitment a reality.

Teams are free to be creative, open, and deeply relational in determining how and where their reparations will be distributed. For example, some teams may choose to form a team pool and distribute/ facilitate/request resources collectively. Others may choose to have each member distribute funds on their own, and possibly keep a shared document tracking the resources flowing through each person. For some teams, this may include resources flowing within a team or between teams.

In order to track and learn from their reparations efforts and experiments, each team is asked to consistently and accurately document their collective reparations resource flow. Each team is free to determine the form this documentation will take.

Recommended practices

- **Ongoing reparations accountability**: Use your regular team meetings to check in with each other about your reparations commitment. Seek support, resources, and inspiration from each other. Keep your commitments alive by finding spaces to talk about them on a regular basis.

- **Reparations commitment for gatherings, trainings, and direct action settings away from home**: When engaged in network-related work away from your home community, if money is pooled to cover expenses, include an appropriate amount for reparations redistribution. Move these resources to local Indigenous and/or Black group(s), as advised by trusted BIPOC friends of the network in that locale.

- **Learning Indigenous lands**: When introducing yourself in new spaces, network members identify the name of the tribe(s) on whose land they reside. Further, we encourage groups to deepen land acknowledgment by learning not just the names of the tribes on whose land you reside, but seeking understanding of those tribes' past and present stories. In this way, active, living relationships of solidarity become possible.

- **Self-education within a team**: This process could include the following:

  o Reclaiming histories of resistance within and across family and ancestral lines—naming the persons and stories of resistance that empower us

  o Pilgrimage to sites with family history of oppression

  o Atonement-centered grief tending, spiritual practice or other ritual observances

  o Intentional liberatory dialogue across racial lines

- **Study and practice together**: There are a wealth of resources available on reparations, and obviously a great deal more on the wider context of racial justice and racial healing. Consider attending a workshop or a lecture together as a team. Read books or watch documentaries together and

organize discussion groups. Engage in self-
guided courses on race together. See "Reparations and Atonement" in the Additional
Resources section of the Appendices for
more.

- **Plan a public event** to openly share, story-
tell, and further explore what it was like
for your team to go through the self-audit
process together, and/or any combination of
the above recommended practices that were
meaningful for your team. What did you learn
about yourselves? What did you decide to do?
What was it like? What suggestions might you
offer to others in your community based on
this experience?

Direct Action

*"More harm can be done through obedience than
through disobedience."*
~ Hannah Arendt ~

We have come together to work against systems of domination
rooted in extraction and exploitation, while supporting the emergence of truly just, life-sustaining alternatives. In defense of life, our
network engages in bold direct action to disrupt the systems driving
racial violence and ecological collapse.

What is direct action
and where does it happen?

> **Direct Action definition** *(adapted from
> Ruckus Society)*: The strategic use of
> immediately effective, disobedient acts
> to achieve a political or social goal and
> challenge an unjust power dynamic. This
> happens at points of intervention through
> embodied practice of nonviolence.[10]

---

10. See the first page of Ruckus Society's *Action Strategy: A How-to Guide*,
https://bit.ly/3u6TYQ9.

The phrase "direct action" is often used and understood interchangeably with "civil disobedience," which implies the breaking of laws and the risk of arrest. While powerful direct actions often include these elements, we have also witnessed and/or carried out "immediately effective, disobedient acts" that do not.

Sometimes the thing we're disobeying is not a law or a government entity, but a custom, narrative, or practice that we feel called to openly and creatively defy. Quite often direct action is a combination of such cultural defiance and civil disobedience.

In short, nonviolent direct action takes many forms, and determining what is most strategic at any moment is subjective.

Our commitment to strategic planning and action

Our network seeks to move **beyond the reactive** and into proactive and transformational action.

```
"If it's not soulful, it's not strategic"
            ~ Movement Generation ~
```

As adrienne marie brown points out in *Emergent Strategy*, "Strategy is a military term simply meaning a plan of action toward a goal." She continues: "Emergent strategies are ways for humans to practice complexity and grow the future through relatively simple interactions." For our network, this means being both **adaptive** and **intentional**.

Intentional action, at its core, moves toward a goal or multiple goals. Naming goals (and consistently revisiting them) is a critical first step in acting strategically.

The Two Hands of Nonviolence

With one hand we say to an oppressor,
or to an unjust system,
'Stop what you are doing.
I refuse to honor the role you are choosing to play.
I refuse to obey you.
I refuse to cooperate with your demands.
I refuse to build the walls and the bombs.
I refuse to pay for the guns.
With this hand I will even interfere
with the wrong you are doing.
I want to disrupt the easy pattern of your life.'

But then the advocate of nonviolence
raises the other hand.
It is raised out-stretched…
With this hand we say,
'I won't let go of you or cast you out of the human race.
I have faith that you can make a better choice
than you are making, and I'll be here
when you are ready.
Like it or not, we are part of one another.'

~ Barbara Deming, *On Revolution and Equilibrium* ~

Action goals are most powerful when they combine disruption of business as usual with embodiment of the world we're longing for. Often the two are so intertwined it's difficult to tell one from the other.

For example, a team's action goals might look something like this:

- Build a powerful sense of unity and possibility among participants

- Work stoppage at our chosen *point of intervention*[11] for eight hours

- Unmask and publicize the violence inherent at the point of intervention

- Publicize alternatives proposed by the impacted community

One-off actions and strategic initiative

Generally speaking, it is best to avoid one-off actions. One-offs rarely make strategic sense and often reinforce a sense of powerlessness in the face of the domination system.

---

11. "A point of intervention is a physical or conceptual place within a system where pressure can be put to disrupt its smooth functioning and push for change." From *Beautiful Trouble*, a global network that supports social movements with strategic tools and training: https://beautifultrouble.org.

There are important exceptions, however. Here are three ways one-off actions may be strategic:

1. **Experimentation:** Recognizing that experimentation is important for creativity and learning, teams will sometimes take action to build skills, test tactics, and/or to explore what it would be like to focus on a specific target. When the primary goal is learning, the use of the action to build power for a sustained campaign may be less imperative. It's still important to be aware of the potential impacts of experimental action on frontline communities, allies, etc.

2. **Emergency response:** Emergency situations might create conditions for the strategic use of one-off actions to merge the power of principled action with public rage, grief, and expression in response to whatever is happening. This might include holding space for public grieving and calls for accountability, for example.

In such moments, strategic analysis may prioritize the need to disrupt immediate harm, to show solidarity, and to prioritize relationships with the most impacted communities.

See below for more on the intersection of direct action and disaster relief/mutual aid.

3. **Solidarity**: Sometimes teams will choose to show up for and with other groups in the context of climate justice and racial justice action. Our multiracial network is particularly committed to supporting calls to action from BIPOC-led groups. Network teams showing up for actions they have not designed themselves are encouraged to refrain from taking a public position on such actions' strategic value (unless leadership has explicitly invited them to help with strategic planning). Teams should be clear with themselves and those around them as to their intentions and commitments (for example, making known our network's commitment to nonviolence), but should not impose—either explicitly or implicitly—their commitments and values on others. Solidarity actions may or may not match our network's theory of change, but strict alignment is not necessary so long as solidarity actions resonate deeply enough with our core values. A team may determine, for example, that a solidarity action will support them to deepen relationships, and will therefore participate in it. Fundamentally, this is about prioritizing relationships and the desire to stand with others above strategic analysis.

Two ways of taking strategic initiative

(strategic initiative = campaigns and other forms of sustained pressure that work together over time to build long-term power to shift/dismantle/transform systems)

1. **Sustained campaigns you build—usually with other groups in coalition.**

   You may begin small and build a coalition, or you may join an existing coalition for the purposes of engaging in a particular campaign that has already been initiated. In either case, if you're engaging as a team, you're doing so as members of the network. *Campaigns are built around a specific goal, ideally a measurable goal, so you'll know if you have achieved it.* It is important to bear in mind that strategic/sustained campaigns to make change may include direct action, but that's not your only tactic. Direct action is one set of powerful tools to use when you believe it can help you achieve your goals.

2. **Your team drops into a one-time action that is part of a strategic, sustained campaign led by others. This is not the same as a "one-off" action.**

When dropping into a campaign initiated by others, even if your team shows up just once for an action you were asked to design/lead or were invited to join, your team can meaningfully contribute to a strategic effort for change. To increase the odds that this will be the case, share your learnings with the organizers (when invited to do so) and follow their lead/vision for the overall effort. In the process, your team will likely generate helpful energy and/or forge important new relationships.

When dropping in to such campaigns, **it is not a team's role to evaluate what is strategic for the campaign or for other groups in the coalition.** The resources offered here are meant to help network teams evaluate their own strategy. If a team is dropping into a campaign, it is because they have identified a strategic reason to do so for themselves.

For example: Your team might be supporting a direct action encampment that is part of the Movement for Black Lives. Your team may think that an encampment is the most strategic use of time, energy, and resources. It is also possible that your team thinks that an encampment is not

```
the best strategic tactic in this context,
but that you determine that showing up
in solidarity represents your longer-term
strategic priority.
```

Taking action at the intersection of climate and racial justice

```
"I am here and so are you. And we matter.
We can change things."
            ~ Ella Baker ~
```

We often focus our interventions on the capitalist fossil fuel economy, by which we mean not only the toxic energy industry that threatens the possibility of sustained life for more and more of Earth's species, but also its various tentacles throughout society. This might mean intervening to disrupt a great variety of harms, such as construction of oil pipelines or new prison facilities, factory farming, low income housing demolition, or the militarization of police. The systems of domination that spin out of these harms reinforce one another, and we seek to transform these systems in ways that knit together our communities, our concerns, and our hopes for the future.

When we show up to take action as a network, we work to bring forward the inseparability of climate and racial justice. We bring racial justice into climate spaces. We bring climate into racial justice spaces. This often means making visible the thing that is less "obvious"—race or Indigenous sovereignty at a pipeline blockade, or climate at a deportation blockade.

We acknowledge that bringing an intersectional analysis into a space can only be done when trust and communication with other groups are robust. These commitments aren't new, and as we live into them, network members are encouraged to embody both curiosity and humility.

Some key considerations related to showing up with an intersectional analysis and awareness:

- <u>When organizing</u>: Choose points of intervention that embody a powerful intersection, and which thoughtfully reinforce that inter-section with one or more of the following: demands, spokespeople, stories, media messaging, art, songs, and what we wear.

  For example: When joining a campaign against an oil pipeline that goes through a disproportionate number of Indigenous and Black communities, the messaging can high-light this injustice as being inseparable from climate impacts.

- <u>When showing up for efforts organized by others</u>: Discernment about what to do and how to do it should be deeply informed by your team's relationships with those who have invited you. This applies to the ways you prepare your hearts and minds, the conversations you engage in, potentially

your art/songs/clothing, and anything you
are specifically invited to do.

For example: When members of a network
team participate in an action focused on
immigrant detention, that team might offer
their vocational calling of song, and if the
offering is received as useful, the team can
check in with leaders concerning which songs
and language(s) are appropriate. A team can
also show up silently in any action roles,
with a willingness to be put to work.

- When in an action space: To foster an honest
  and humble frame of mind, consider your own
  patterns of complicity and evaluate the ways
  that you fuel the things that you are struggling against.

- In all settings, take care to avoid preachi-
  ness of any kind, but especially in relation
  to climate in spaces more squarely focused
  on racial justice. We endeavor to embody our
  intersectional analysis by showing up and
  being who we are as a network. At the end of
  the day, how we show up and the strength of
  our practices will be the message we most
  powerfully convey.

As teams, our commitment to act in defense of life—slowing down
species extinction; protecting the water, air, and soil; and taking
down police brutality, mass incarceration and mass deportation—is

at the center of our shared efforts. When we show up to organize or to participate in an action, campaign, or other kind of event, we strive to build upon the foundation of this core commitment.

> "The struggle for freedom
> is the next best thing
> to actually being free."
> ~ Lean Alejandro ~

Emotional release, protest and direct action

Protesting, demonstrating, and resisting are often used as a ways to express the rage and pain of living within the domination system. While emotional expression is an essential part of who we are, and having outlets for our feelings is deeply important, we want to be careful that our actions are not limited to that. This is not to say that we should put our emotions on hold when we step into action. Far from it. This is simply a reminder, an important one, that when we're planning for action, and engaged in action, we want to stay focused on our broader goals.

For our network it has been helpful to consider the following distinction between protest and direct action:

Protest: Requesting and/or demanding that those in power use their power differently. (Often driven by a **SHUT IT DOWN** energy.)

Direct Action: Cultivating and bringing forth a power from within that allows us to build collective power for ourselves, which we employ in service to life. (Counterbalances **SHUT IT DOWN** with the addition of a spirit of **OPEN IT UP**)

Protest and **Direct Action** will cross-pollinate and are often both present in actions in which we participate (along with a good measure of emotional release, too). Be that as it may, asking ourselves, **"What is the value of this action in relation to co-creating the overall movement?"** is at the heart of our commitment to strategic planning.

Is a "riot" strategic?

A politician or military official may answer, "no, not ever." But we know that uprisings, such as those which took place across the United States in the wake of George Floyd's murder in June of 2020, can be powerfully influential. Such actions may not cohere to a detailed campaign plan or build toward a carefully considered set of outcomes, but they should not be underestimated as potential catalysts for change. Uprisings make space for expressions of rage and grief. And sometimes they create conditions that awaken an entire society to the oppression and violence to which particular communities are subjected every day.

While our network is fully committed to nonviolence, we also do not support the oversimplified condemnation and moral judgment against violent uprisings by marginalized communities. These uprisings are the result of centuries of systemic violence that has gone unaddressed. Strategic or not, they are oftentimes a cry for peace from a community that has never had it, and criticisms of these actions tend to come from communities of relative privilege.

While violent uprisings can bring about significant cultural change and give voice to a community who has never had it, we also acknowledge that violent uprisings do not give us the means to heal and strengthen broken relationships. Ultimately, it is this healing and strengthening work that our network is called to engage in.

In the final analysis, a riot is the language of the unheard. And what is it that America has failed to hear? … It has failed to hear that the promises of freedom and justice have not been met. And it has failed to hear that large segments of white society are more concerned about tranquility and the status quo than about justice, equality, and humanity. And so in a real sense our nation's summers of riots are caused by our nation's winters of delay. And as long as America postpones justice, we stand in the position of having these recurrences of violence and riots over and over again.

~Martin Luther King Jr.,
"The Other America," 1967~

Because direct action is a craft—we encourage practitioners to be learners. In the Appendices, you will find a sampling of tools to support you to dig deeper and build your skill set. And, for much more, see the FVN Direct Action Manual, available at: https://bit.ly/3qKd7aM

Where are the "frontlines"?

The term "frontlines" is commonly used in organizing spaces, and we find it important to clarify what it means for our network. Contrary to what many think, a place where an action is happening is not necessarily the "frontlines."

Frontline communities are those that are directly impacted, that have disproportionately had land/health/wealth/labor/resources extracted or stolen, and that have also been able to collectively name the ways they are burdened and are organizing for action together.[12]

Some teams in our network will be rooted in frontline communities; some will not. A team's work will be largely shaped by this distinction.

Impacted communities "experience 'first and worst,' the consequences of climate change. These are communities of color and low-income communities, whose neighborhoods often lack basic

---

12. See page 13 of Hilary Moore and Joshua Kahn Russell's "Organizing Cools the Planet: Tools and Reflections to Navigate the Climate Crisis." https://bit.ly/3j1cWlL

infrastructure and who will be increasingly vulnerable as our climate deteriorates."[13]

- We believe that frontline and impacted communities are **powerful** and where the most trustworthy solutions come from.

- We encourage teams who are not rooted in frontline communities to orient themselves to show up in solidarity and receive leadership and direction from these communities, and to support their ongoing work and campaigns.

- We know that some impacted and frontline communities have been so burned by outsiders that the presence of a team from the outside can be received with hesitation (especially in the case of predominantly white teams).

The intersection of direct action and disaster relief/mutual aid

As the impacts of climate change intensify, our direct action teams will likely find themselves increasingly drawn into, invited into, and forced into spaces where the work looks more like disaster relief

---

13. Holland, Carolyn. "Centering Frontline Communities." https://bit.ly/3NIG2aj.

than what we usually think of as direct action. This transition will be a deeply significant one for our network as we learn how to face crises together.

Our direct action commitment is not founded on a naive hope that we can somehow prevent major climate-driven upheaval, whether or not we call it or conceptualize it as "collapse." Our direct action commitment is founded on our desire to serve life by honoring and protecting it to the best of our ability.

"Mutual aid is when people get together to meet each other's basic survival needs with a shared understanding that the systems we live under are not going to meet our needs and we can do it together RIGHT NOW!"
~ Big Door Brigade ~

Mutual aid is a kind of direct action. While it does not usually fall into the kind of disruptive direct action that this network is inviting, we anticipate that some of the direct action we engage in the coming years will also be in some shape or form mutual aid. Mutual aid is a threat to the entire system of individualism and coercion because it is a deep commitment to reciprocity. *Simply put, mutual aid is the direct act of loving and being loved back.*

Relationship with police

"No one can be authentically human while he
prevents others from being so."
~ Paulo Freire, Pedagogy of the Oppressed ~

Every community needs safety and systems of accountability that reflect the values and vision of how they want to be in the world and with one another. The criminal justice system in the United States utterly fails to fulfill this purpose. The criminal justice system does, however, serve to protect and maintain an inherently unjust and destructive status quo. It is the state's apparatus for maintaining and exerting control through the use and threat of state violence.

This takes many forms, including harassment, racial profiling, criminalization of poverty, physical violence, deportation, and incarceration. Police forces in many parts of the US arose from efforts to maintain slaveholder "property."[14] Today, police forces are the criminal justice system's first line of enforcers. As such, they represent the racism, classism, and otherization that characterize the system they serve, and they are charged with carrying out violence on behalf of the state. This is the role police officers have taken on, regardless of the fact that most carry it out with a genuine concern for the common good, and that police officers often carry out difficult and necessary tasks in service to their communities.

Because of the particular legacy of racism and the way it continues to manifest in US society, we—as a group committed to direct action—need to speak to the role of the criminal justice system, and police specifically.

---

14. For more on the history of U.S. policing and its relationship to slavery, please see www.bit.ly/3p1dCFM or www.bit.ly/3jPpgYv.

We resist the temptation to dehumanize others, including police. This is an extremely difficult task given that dehumanization is part of the fabric of our society.

The system of policing is one that relies on violence, fear, repression and a colonizer mentality. But the individuals who are employed to enforce that mentality are human beings with a human psyche, just like any other. It's silly to assume that these men and women aren't impacted by the violence they witness and participate in every day. No human being can participate in the levels of heightened violence that police are engaged in without being affected by it…

Individual accountability requires healing, and a space for the perpetrator of the harm to feel remorse for their actions. I've learned over time that people can't empathize with the pain that they caused until their own pain and story have been honored. So, can we build a movement that honors the pain of the officers and creates spaces to help them see the pain that they cause?

~ Kazu Haga, *Policing Isn't Working for Cops Either* ~

Police violence is a reality in the lives of many people and a major part of the history of this country. There is widespread distrust and fear of police, especially among Black, Indigenous, transgender people, immigrants, and poor people of every race. It is vital that network teams seek to deeply understand this reality and to reflect together about what it means in terms of how they want to show up within the wider movement ecosystem.

We believe we must draw hard lines for ourselves, refusing to use the tools of violent oppressors—namely, in this case, dehumanizing whole groups of people, including people who interpret reality differently than we do. Those tactics have been practiced for thousands of years to justify murder, genocide, and racism.

Some essential guidelines:

- When working with other groups, make space for and invite them to share about their past experiences with police, their orientation toward police, and their wishes in terms of the role your team will play. In order to maximize the feeling of safety and solidarity, endeavor to show up with as much congruence to the wishes of the organizing community as possible, and hold sensitivity about how your team's preferred way of interacting with police might impact others beyond your team.

- Our network is committed to not answering dehumanization with dehumanization and to practicing solidarity with individuals, groups, and communities who have been most

```
impacted by police violence. Teams are
responsible for interacting with police in
ways that accord with network values.
```

In the event that a team is not able to authentically live up to another groups' standards of allyship, the team may discern that they cannot with integrity commit to a partnership with that group. The team's process of determining this needs to be taken seriously, with an eye to their own egos and, as applicable, their privilege. Is the other group's expectation a real barrier to collaboration because it would require you to go against a core principle, or does it represent a request that would be difficult or uncomfortable to meet? If a team determines that there is a real barrier, this should be communicated with transparency, honesty, and humility. **We are not here to tell others how to do their movement work**.

This part of our DNA is necessarily going to be a work in progress, including learning from ongoing experience and from deep listening and conversation with others. We are going to make and learn from our mistakes.

Considerations for arrest

Given our network's commitment to direct action, when deemed necessary, our members will risk arrest and time in state custody. If we are going to opt into the criminal justice system, we want to do so responsibly, acknowledging the relative privilege we have embodied or claimed by voluntarily putting ourselves in a position where we may be charged with an offense.

One way to do this responsibly is to take the time and emotional energy to witness how the system treats other people who didn't choose to be there. Most of the other people who will be in the courtroom with you are going to be unhappy to be there. We encourage you to treat these people and their cases with respect. Examples of ways to do this include avoiding conversation with one another while other people's cases are being heard, and keeping your group's demeanor determined, serious, and focused.

Much more on this and many related topics can be found in the FVN Direct Action Manual: `https://bit.ly/3qKd7aM`.

Core Practice:
21 days of direct action

Each network team commits to engaging in direct action at the intersection of racial and climate justice for a minimum of 21 days each calendar year. The network provides this quantification to support teams in bringing this work off the page and into the world.

What counts as an action day?

We trust that teams joining this network are deeply called to be taking action on behalf of life. We are a decentralized network, and there is no national entity that will be tracking whether you have met a commitment.

As a general guideline, the network holds that **an action day is a day when a critical mass of your team collectively directs their labor toward an action.**

When a critical mass of your team strategically directs
energy toward:

- A day of preparation for an action you are
  leading or participating in, such as an art
  build, scouting, final planning meetings or
  training specific to the action

- The actual day(s) when the action takes
  place

- Days of jail time and/or jail support time
  following the action

A team action day likely isn't:

- A day when you have meetings or trainings
  not specific to a particular action

- A day of travel

- A day when one or two people from your
  team are at an action, but the team hasn't
  collectively organized around it

- A day when you're at an action without a
  clear strategic reason for being there as a
  network team[15]

If, after considering the above criteria, your team is still unsure
whether a particular day should count toward your team's 21 days of
action, consider this more intuitive indicator:

On the morning of the day in question, did you wake up thinking,
**"I know in my heart that today is a day my team is
taking action together."**

> Vocation is integral to this network. We
> want to bring people of varied gifts into
> direct action spaces. Our network is not
> interested in sending only "activist
> types" into actions.
>
> **Whoever you are, there is a place for
> you here.** On action days, some team
> members may remain home to care for
> children, do remote digital support or
> coordinate legal strategy. Perhaps the
> people who traditionally would be at
> the action itself will grow into these
> kinds of support roles, to free up those
> who usually stay home.

---

15. The network DNA doesn't prescribe strategy but rather encourages each team
to determine what they believe to be strategic. There are many resources in the
Appendices, as well as the FVN Direct Action Manual that may support you in this
discernment: https://bit.ly/3qKd7aM.

Remember: Not all direct actions involve risking arrest. And yet, every disruptive action that seeks to transform injustice does carry some form of risk.

Part of our work to dismantle individualism and hero culture is to view **all roles and gifts** as valuable. There are people who face greater risk when they take disruptive action: people who are undocumented or have tenuous immigration status, single parents, or formerly incarcerated people, for example. As a network, we recognize that a true community of resistance values its members as whole people, and we celebrate vocation—the diverse gifts each of us bring to the network community.

For the purpose of self-accountability regarding the 21-day action commitment, you are invited to keep track of your team action days. An **action log** can help you keep track, and can also be a valuable resource as you reflect upon your team's work at any annual retreat or day of reflection your team may plan. You can ask: Are we taking action in the world to an extent that reflects our deep desire to see real change in society? If not, what barriers or outstanding needs are blocking us from doing so, and how might we call on our community of support or new team members to help us address them?

Fierce Vulnerability

"We need a movement that has the courage to have a
relationship with our heartbrokenness."
~ Rev. Lynice Pinkard ~

Our exploration of fierce vulnerability is ongoing and our understanding of it continues to deepen. Here are some of the ways we've attempted to describe it thus far:

First, some of the language from the first edition of our network's zine, published in the summer of 2018:

> *Vulnerability is our strength—made evident as a lived combination of love, truthfulness, and courageous action.*
>
> *We recognize the need to excavate the dark and forgotten places in our hearts, to heal from past and present traumas, and to embrace restoration and reconciliatory practices with one another, in order to show up to this work well and empowered. We make space for our heartbreak and anger, uncertainty and regret. For our joy, wonder, laughter, tenderness, grief and praise…*

As we act to honor, uplift, and defend life, we are committed to taking and holding the initiative. We show up authentically, standing for what we believe in, with strength and firm resolve, and with openness, love, and respect for all we encounter. This love for all is expressed without timidity or deference to those who would exploit or demean us and others…

We seek to lovingly hold one another accountable to the ways we ourselves cause both personal harm and systemic exploitation. We center the building of trust and love among us, knowing that ultimately the strength of our relationships with one another will be the measure of our contribution to the movement.

Our network is coming together to respond to a level of violence and destruction unprecedented in human history. And we know that counterbalancing a massive escalation requires an equally massive response.

And yet, our time in direct action movements has shown us that too often when we escalate our tactics of nonviolent direct action, we also have a tendency to escalate the binary "us vs. them/right vs. wrong" worldview. This is a worldview that ultimately grows out of the delusion of separation—the very thing that is destroying the fabric of our society and our planet's ecosystems.

Trauma is a defining characteristic of our times. Whether it's the collective trauma we experience as a result of the climate emergency, the intergenerational trauma that so many of us carry within our family histories, or any number of other forms of trauma, our nervous systems are understandably unregulated. And we know from experience that when our bodies are in the fight, flight, or freeze of a trauma response, our minds are apt to gravitate to the counterproductive binaries mentioned above.

We believe there is a different way, a way to harness our power and stop the wheels of injustice in their tracks, without questioning the dignity of all people; a way to escalate our tactics while doubling down on relationship; a way to engage in direct action as a modality of collective trauma healing. Fierce vulnerability is the name we've given to this different way.

Our network embraces the term "fierce vulnerability" to honor many lineages of nonviolent struggle that have shaped our work.

At the same time, it is vital to acknowledge that the framing of nonviolence has often been used to discredit and undermine actions taken by Black and Indigenous peoples to protect their communities from violence.

Our network holds a commitment to a fierce tradition of nonviolent action that does not shame, cast judgment, or indulge in moralizations about the choices of others. This tradition employs nonviolence as a tool of liberation and therefore eschews all forms of complicity with oppression.

Fierce vulnerability and the human nervous system

Fierce vulnerability provides an umbrella for essential fields and practices not usually associated with nonviolence, such as neurobiology, trauma healing, and grief tending. In the face of social and ecological collapse, these fields and their relationship with nonviolent direct action are of paramount importance to our network. Serious training and discipline have long characterized the practice of nonviolence, but until recently these other closely related frameworks have not.

Both in our teams and in our direct action, we will undoubtedly have moments of tension and challenge, and perhaps even moments of intense physical and/or emotional confrontation. Contemporary understandings of neurobiology and trauma can help us greatly to navigate such moments in ways that care for our safety and the safety of others, as well as supporting the effectiveness of the actions we are taking.

When humans perceive threat, we experience some degree of reactivity, from minor to extreme states of fight (anger, elevated heart rate), flight (anxiety, elevated heart rate), freeze (getting numb or going blank, elevated or reduced heart rate), blame (persistent belief that others are "wrong" or "the problem," accompanied by anger or frustration), or shame (persistent belief that there is something "wrong" with us), etc. When in such reactive states, our outlook on our situation narrows, we lose our ability to hold complexity and nuance, and we are less able to make optimal choices and to connect effectively with others.

Furthermore, when we are reactive, the people we engage with are much more likely to become reactive in turn, whether they are our fellow team members, the police, or anyone else. In this way, our own reactivity tends to further escalate conflict, which ultimately undermines both the effectiveness and integrity of our work.

This does not mean we have to give up on our intensity. Our passion is a gift. When combined with the ability to ground and regulate our nervous system, our powerful emotions are essential to fueling our action and connecting effectively with ourselves and others as we act.

As we learn to regulate our nervous systems and relax reactive patterns in the short term, and to heal the trauma underlying these patterns in the long term, we increase coherence in our brain and have more access to our underlying capacity for courage, creativity, inner calm, and compassion for ourselves and others. This essential capacity is referred to in various psychological modalities and spiritual/religious traditions by names such as the Self, witness consciousness, the ground of being, Buddha nature, Christ consciousness, etc.

When we are grounded in this essential capacity for compassion and courage, we are able to "respond" rather than "react" in confrontational situations—to stand up boldly to protect life, while still keeping our hearts open to the shared humanity of those who may oppose us. For this reason, supporting short-term nervous system regulation and long-term trauma healing—in ourselves and others—is one of the most essential aspects of fierce vulnerability.

More on trauma
and trauma healing

> If you are convinced that ending white
> supremacy begins with social and polit-
> ical action, do not read this book unless
> you are willing to be challenged. We need
> to begin with the healing of trauma
> in dark-skinned bodies, light-skinned
> bodies, our neighborhoods and communi-
> ties, and the law enforcement profes-
> sion. Social and political actions are
> essential, but they need to be part of
> a larger strategy of healing, justice,
> and creating room for growth in trauma-
> tized flesh-and-blood bodies.
>
> ~ Resmaa Menakem, from the introduction to
> *My Grandmother's Hands* ~

Everyone experiences difficult situations, and some of us experience many more than others. If these difficult situations include significant violence, shame, fear, isolation, or pain, they will likely result in trauma, especially if they are not processed in supportive environments. Trauma can be caused by long-term harsh relationships and isolated acute events, as well as by systemic oppression, such as racism, homophobia, sexism, poverty, and stress caused by ongoing climate disruption. A quickly growing body of research also shows that trauma is passed down from generation to generation, meaning that the level of trauma suffered by our ancestors is hard-wired into our DNA.

The various forms of trauma that we carry in our bodies resurface when triggered by new events. Understandably, such experiences tend to be more frequent in diverse settings, where old or more recent wounds are reactivated around charged identity fault lines such as race, gender identity and expression, class, physical ability, religion, sexual orientation, and other aspects of personal and group identity.

The work of trauma healing is absolutely essential in our fractured society, and especially so for a network committed to racial healing. Trauma healing is deep work which can take many forms. Teams are encouraged to read "Five Opportunities for Healing and Making Room for Growth," by Resmaa Menakem (in the Appendices) for helpful suggestions. Menakem's work de-stigmatizes trauma, while also creating healthy boundaries about the level of care and expertise required for different types of healing work. In short, individuals can do some trauma work on their own, some of it can be directly supported by team members without in-depth training, and some will require the aid of skilled trauma healers and/or the structure of carefully designed programs.

We therefore encourage teams to carefully self-assess their capacities. Teams without strong trauma healing skills and capacity are encouraged to identify the trauma healers and trauma healing resources available in their network community, and in the wider community at large. Developing working relationships with trauma healers is essential, so that teams can call on them when the trauma of team members or others in the network community is more than a team is able to responsibly tend.

We further encourage teams to develop the extremely valuable skill of lovingly acknowledging moments when a presenting trauma is more than a team can handle. In such cases it is vital that a team takes action to find another time and space, and to enlist the needed help, in order to tend to the person(s) whose trauma has been activated. It is equally vital that the team honors the person experiencing the trauma by offering empathy, and resisting any tendency toward fixing, minimizing, or shaming.

Fierce vulnerability and integral nonviolence

"Integral nonviolence" denotes **a transformative approach to personal, social, and systemic change**, rather than the widely accepted understanding of nonviolence as a tactical rejection of the use of physical force in situations of conflict. The iceberg model discussed earlier (see section titled "An Integral Approach Geared Toward Direct Action") highlights the three deeply interwoven parts of our integral nonviolence commitment: self-transformation, community uplift, and direct action.

We recognize that for all practical purposes—in the human realm at least—pure, unadulterated nonviolence does not exist. We have come into this world at the height of consumer-capitalism, industrial plunder, technologization, oppression, colonization, and ecocide. Under these circumstances it's difficult to imagine any given situation or conflict that we could approach with pure nonviolence.

Our network sees nonviolence, therefore, as a powerful beacon and guide, but not as a badge to be worn or a mission that can ever be fully accomplished. That said, members of our network are firmly committed to an ongoing, disciplined process of moving consistently and deliberately in the direction of greater love and greater courage, which we understand to be the essence of nonviolence.

Integral Nonviolence:
Three Examples of a Three-fold Approach
(incorporating self-transformation, community uplift, and direct action)

1. Oceti Sakowin Camp at Standing Rock:

- A hub for months of powerful frontlines direct action

- An alternative mini-society where thousands of water protectors self-organized to meet their collective food, shelter, and health needs

- Grounded by prayer, singing, and ceremony

2. The African American Freedom Movement (usually referred to the Civil Rights Movement):

- Catalyzed mass nation-changing direct action campaigns like those in Montgomery, Birmingham, and Selma

- Strengthened by deep-rooted, ongoing community organizing throughout the South

- Fueled by the songs, spirituality and fellowship of the Black church

3. The Salt Satyagraha in India:

- Set off mass civil disobedience throughout the nation for a full year

- Centered on the reclamation of salt processing, an ancient indigenous industry monopolized by the British Empire

- Initiated by a sacred pilgrimage carried forward by 78 members of a spiritual community

This network holds that a direct action tradition rooted in fierce vulnerability is a powerful tool for healing at the personal, social, and systemic levels. We believe that the principles and healing practices that are impactful at the smallest scale will be impactful at the largest scale—and everywhere in between.

While the shape it takes varies due to our social positionality and our vocations, integral nonviolence calls us to steadily renounce our extractive and exploitative ways of inhabiting this planet, in favor of strengthening and exercising our capacity for earth-centered, eco-resilient living.

This shift represents a prime example of the overlap between self-transformation and community uplift. Members of our network are engaged in a wide range of experiments in pursuit of this aspiration, such as abstaining from cars and planes, using candlelight instead of electric light, using composting toilet systems, growing and distributing healthy food, and avoiding or limiting cell phone and computer ownership and use.

It is vital to acknowledge that the prospect of experimentation along these lines looks very different to different communities because of colonialism, past and present. For those most often on the receiving end of the domination system's oppression, getting up and out into the world each day, in the face of the onslaught of racism, patriarchy, and colonization, without losing heart or surrendering one's dignity, is powerful nonviolence in and of itself.

The goal of nonviolence is to stop repeating cycles of harm and separation. Ultimately, this happens through healing. In this network, we start the healing process by looking into ourselves and noticing how we perpetuate harm in and through our lives. We acknowledge that the harm we cause against ourselves or others is really an attempt to meet a universal human need, even if the strategies we use end up leaving more unmet needs than when we began.

Reckoning with, accounting for, and grieving the harm we perpetuate creates a pathway for further steps. By developing patience, acceptance, genuine love for ourselves, and by processing past trauma—as discussed above, the healing process continues. Ultimately this healing is what makes us capable of ending cycles of harm in our personal lives. This is the self-transformation work which provides the foundation for the type of community uplift and direct action work we long to do. This is a long transformational process involving body, mind, and spirit. It requires hard work and a supportive community.

Nonviolent campaigns in this network reach toward the wholeness of everyone involved. The process described above is the same process we have in mind as we move into the public sphere to stop cycles of harm perpetuated by others.

We see nonviolent action, therefore, as healing action. Nonviolence acknowledges cycles of harm and the challenges that each and every person faces in breaking free of those cycles. Nonviolence acknowledges that behind every act of harm lies a legitimate need that someone is trying to meet. While we strive to be uncompromising in our commitment to stopping harm, we simultaneously strive to remember that there are unmet needs embedded in that harm, and that those needs are important. This is often incredibly difficult, but the more healing we have experienced in ourselves, the more we will be able to reach out to others with this type of compassionate accountability.

A nonviolence foundation[16]

- Nonviolence is active and courageous, not passive.

- When we act in a loving and truthful way, we make ourselves vulnerable. This kind of vulnerability has power.

- Nonviolence is not merely a tactic to be picked up or put down depending on the circumstances.

- Nonviolence is a practical interpersonal skill. We build it through learning to interact with each other nonviolently. We

---

16. Several of these points were adapted from the Six Principles of Kingian Nonviolence Conflict Reconciliation, as described in the *The Leaders Manual: A Structured Guide and Introduction to Kingian Nonviolence: The Philosophy and Methodology*, Institute for Human Rights and Responsibilities, 1995.

work to stop seeing each other as enemies, even when it's difficult.

- "Committing to nonviolence" is not the same as the ability to act nonviolently. The difference here is deeply significant. One's ability to act nonviolently is hard to self-assess. Feedback from others is essential.

- Nonviolence is developed through daily practice in building the skills of empathy, love, patience, and honesty in a practical way in our daily lives. Without such practice, our ability to act nonviolently will be minimal.

- Nonviolence is grounded in the belief that no one is truly, fully liberated until all beings are liberated. There is no "winner" and no "victory" apart from this reality.

- Nonviolence distinguishes injustice from persons behaving unjustly. It calls us to cease identifying each other as enemies and to refuse the oppressive tactic of dehumanization. Our opposition is directed at systems of oppression and destruction, not at individuals or their personalities.

- Nonviolent action means taking strategic initiative to create change, not merely reacting to outside forces or events.

- When we feel led to persuade and enlighten, we do our best to remain willing and ready to also be persuaded and enlightened.

- Nonviolence invites paradox. We cannot have answers to all the questions and contradictions that emerge.

- Experimentation in nonviolent action is sacred work.

- This nonviolence foundation is a gift given by a long line of practitioners and movement builders who came before us. We honor lineages of direct action, fierce vulnerability, and integral nonviolence by doing our own experimenting, learning, and growing, in loving, courageous service to life.

The field

Consider the difference :

```
Slowly entering a silent circle of
towering redwoods.


Rushing through a bustling, booming
construction site.


                . . .


Waiting in line under buzzing fluores-
cent lights at the DMV.


Sitting with loved ones around a
candlelit dinner table.
```

In any given situation, everything physical, along with the mindsets, intentions, actions, and relationships of those present, contributes to an energetic field.

You can feel this in everyday interactions: Walking into a room where an argument was previously happening, stumbling upon a tender moment between two people—this field is something generated between all of us, and it can be tapped into.

In direct action spaces, tapping into the field can be both transformative and strategic. Transformative because a field of deep seriousness, or joy, or power has the potential to change those who experience it. Strategic because the field can hold so much of the vision and tone desired for that particular space. Sometimes a field so powerfully invokes the world as we want it that that world becomes tangible enough to touch. It impacts us on the level of our central nervous system, which tracks both safety and belonging. The experience sticks. We experience grace.

When we participate in direct action we strive for connection and transformation in and between people, no matter their role or stance. This includes the wider audience that hears about such actions after the fact. The confrontations and risk-taking our teams take part in underscore the necessity of practices that center love. Such practices enable us to influence the field in ways that reflect what's true for us.

The field is shaped by everything we do. There is no separating our impact on the field from the quality of our relationships (others can tell when you show up with friends vs. colleagues), and our capacities as individuals and teams to show up with compassionate and courageous presence. **It is just as vital to attend to the field during our team meetings as it is when we're in direct action spaces.** Transformation is fractal. We can't expect to help generate a transformative and healing field in public spaces if the field in our team meetings is ungrounded or shot through with resentment.

It is also important to acknowledge that different circumstances call for different types of field work. Sometimes we'll want to inject humor into the field, other times solemnity. Sometimes the occasion will call for righteous indignation, sometimes for grief, sometimes for celebration. Sometimes an action or a campaign will call for an interweaving of many expressions. We tune our spirits and our field practices accordingly. We experiment and see what we learn.

Field first aid: Many of us have experienced how delicate the field can be in action spaces. One yell, one chant, one sign, one interaction can immediately bring about a sense of separation and the emotional signature of "us vs. them." As disorienting as this can be, it helps to not view this as a disaster. When the field is disrupted, we adapt and do what we can to move it back in the direction we want it to go.

If necessary, we do this again and again (and again and again). In some situations a fairly high-level de-escalation intervention might be required. Often enough, however, a certain well-placed (and hopefully well-sung) song will do the trick. Or perhaps silence will be the needed field first aid. Sometimes it's an unexpected act of generosity or playfulness that will help recalibrate the field. The more acquainted a team is with its field toolbox the better, and, whenever there's time for it, it's good to seek advice from your teammates before tinkering with your disrupted field.

Field first aid is a particular and powerful vocational calling. It sometimes emerges at unlikely times and from unlikely sources. Keep an eye out for it among your teammates and those with whom you stand in solidarity. It can show up as spiritual leadership, an uplifting and inspiring presence, or an energetic connection that binds. When vocation is honored within a team, field tending is one of the gifts that will likely emerge in actions and other spaces.

The field and technology use: When it comes to helping generate the field we long to act in, we recognize that there is no substitute for one another's presence—that is, one another's physical, touchable, real time presence. In support of connection, belonging, and creating a field conducive to heart-centered work, we therefore prioritize in-person connections whenever possible. We do not default to the organizing norms of the dominant culture (i.e., habitual cell-phone usage, computers for note taking, unnecessary PowerPoint and social media as standard organizing tools).

Tech and direct action: We encourage conversation and decision-making about tech use before taking action together, including with other teams or organizations your team may be collaborating with. We encourage our teams to make mindful, deliberate choices about tech use, and to know that these choices will deeply influence the fields in which we do our work.

The network holds as a recommended guideline that no more than one person per team will be plugged into their devices during actions, and that other members not bring their devices.

Tech-free meeting spaces: Teams are asked to hold their meetings and gatherings tech free, meaning that phones, computers, and other tech gadgets are not brought into the meeting/gathering space, and notes are taken by hand (and are either typed up later, stored digitally as a photo, or simply organized in an old school notebook or binder) when possible. This commitment pertains to meetings and gatherings of all kinds—training, planning, visioning, decision-making, debriefing, fun and fellowship. (See the Decision-Making section for more on tech-free meeting spaces.)

Relationship to security culture

While our network's orientation to transparency and security culture will be different from that of many other movement groups, it is important for network members to have a baseline understanding of "security culture."

Security culture is often deemed as necessary to protect the individuals and groups participating in direct action, especially those groups that are routinely targeted by state violence—people of marginalized identities.

But often, sadly, security culture ends up undermining itself, replicating the same isolation and separation that we are attempting to dismantle in the first place.

Because of our commitment to fierce vulnerability and because of the type of field we hope to help generate in direct action spaces, we prioritize a culture of transparency over a culture of security. In practical terms this means that as a general rule we do not use encryption for network communication, "mask up,"[17] or engage in other measures typically associated with security culture.

On occasion a team may choose deliberately to use encryption because (1) its use would be tactically important to plan and pull off an action that requires enough surprise to be effective, and/or (2) the team is collaborating with other groups in the wider movement ecosystem that use encryption either as a matter of course, or are doing so for a particular action or campaign.

In the end, it will be up to each team to make informed decisions together about their norms with regard to transparency and security culture and when it may be appropriate to ramp up security measures. In general, we are committed to being as transparent as possible.

We anticipate that standards of security culture will be set with regard to the social position of team members experiencing or anticipating violence at the hands of the state or other actors.

---

17 . This general rule is a response to security culture norms. It does not apply to wearing masks for health reasons (e.g. during a global pandemic).

Core Practice:
quarterly reflection circles

Our ability to practice fierce vulnerability and to build the type of field that we believe will bring about transformation requires us to do deep inner and interpersonal healing work.

The *quarterly reflection circle* is a heartfelt interpersonal feedback process with the intention to contribute to the growth and celebration of each team member, to support their capacity to contribute to their community and its purpose, and to build up our muscles for radical honesty and fierce vulnerability with one another.

We envision reflection circles as a full-day or even multi-day event, with each person on the team having roughly an hour to share and listen. This is an opportunity for your team to spend a spacious amount of time together, to break bread together, and to deepen in relationship together. We invite teams to bring in other network practices to these circles to help build the desired field. These might include singing, starting each round with silence, meeting outdoors or by candlelight.

All members of the team will take turns being the "focus person," and will begin with a self-reflection round. This is an opportunity for you, the focus person, to reflect on your contributions, growth edges, challenges and barriers to the purpose and values of the community. This is followed by a round of circle reflections, where you as the focus person have an opportunity to hear from each member of your team about how they have perceived you showing up in the team, in the network, and in the world. You will then have an opportunity to reflect back to the circle about what you heard from them. Finally, you will work with your team to create and commit to an action plan, integrating your own reflections with the feedback from your teammates.

In addition to each member having their own round, the team as a whole will have its own team round at least annually, with each member reflecting on the team as a whole—what am I celebrating about this team? What am I challenged by? How have we, as a team, contributed to the values and goals of the network? This will also be followed by the creation of a team action plan.

All newly forming network teams and collectives whose work is ongoing are asked to initiate a reflection circle within the first 2 months of their formation, and from then on on an every 3-month basis.

More details on suggested structures and format for these reflection circles can be found in the Appendices.

Recommended practices

- **Self-regulation and trauma healing practices**

  o **Empathic listening/co-counseling:**
    Regularly take equal time with another
    person to practice empathic listening,
    drawing on modalities such as Nonviolent
    Communication, Re-evaluation Counseling,
    etc. with particular attention to where
    healing is needed in order to show up for
    the work of racial healing and direct
    action. With attention to vocation, have
    one person research one or more of these
    methods and facilitate at least three
    trial runs of them with your team. (At
    least three so the team really gets a
    sense for the method.) Debrief and eval-
    uate. If one of these methods is proving
    helpful, keep going with it.

  o ***My Grandmother's Hands* group
    study and practice.** Organize a weekly
    or bi-weekly book group to share the
    learning and hands-on somatic practices
    offered in *My Grandmother's Hands* by
    Resmaa Menakem. This will support the
    healing of trauma related to racism, and
    specifically to the impacts of white body
    supremacy on white folks, Black folks and

police officers. This may not be as relevant for other BIPOC members.

o **Meditation**: Try 10 minutes a week of
team meditation together. Meditation is
recognized by many wisdom traditions as
well as scientific research as an essential tool in self-regulation and trauma
healing. In addition to various spiritual traditions of meditation, there are
secular approaches as well, including
Interpersonal Neurobiology (IPNB) and
Mindfulness Based Stress Reduction
(MBSR) (see Additional Resources for
more).

o **Grief and rage tending**: Hold grief
tending and rage tending circles. Bring
in a skilled facilitator within or
outside the network for the first year
of this practice in order to learn the
techniques. (Despite good intentions,
attempting to do such deep work without
expertise may cause harm.) As a complement to this practice, sharing our feelings in a structured form in the presence
of caring team members can be a powerful
component of your healing journey.

- **Sharing celebrations and learning**

  o Schedule time together to share about your adventures and accomplishments in the realm of **self-transformation**, through story-telling, skillshares, support circles, etc. A helpful prompt: How is our inner work moving us to renounce the domination system in practical, observable ways in our personal lives?

  o Schedule time together to share about your adventures and accomplishments in the realm of **community uplift**, through story-telling, presentations, hands-on skill shares, site visits, etc. A helpful prompt: What are our day-to-day community-based practices for saying "no" to the domination system and "yes" to the world we long to inhabit?

- **Loving-kindness meditation**: A practice that comes from the Buddhist tradition, where it is referred to as Metta Practice.[18]

- **Multi-day silent meditation/nature retreats**: An immersion in "healthy silence"

---

18. https://www.mettainstitute.org/mettameditation.html

with skillful facilitators/teachers can be
extremely helpful in the healing process.
Short periods of silence on a daily/weekly
basis can help maintain psycho-spiritual
well-being while long retreats can help
reveal deeply held patterns/stories and
hidden traumas.

- **Fasting**: Occasional fasting with respect to
food or speech has helped several members of
the network. This can help to release things
that are stuck, to clarify priorities, and
to come into alignment with one's deepest
values. Some network members have engaged in
fasts from various forms of technology, such
as planes, cars, computers, internet, email,
cell and smartphones, and electric light.
For some members, such fasts have been a
gateway to giving up some of these things
entirely.

- **Being mindful of our ecological footprints
and responding through action**: Seek
and practice meaningful expressions of a
balanced and regenerative relationship with
the Earth.

Recommended practices for tending to the field

- **Verbal de-escalation**: Get training as a team in verbal de-escalation practices (for the purpose of not letting police and counter-protestors control the field and general action safety).

- **Action ritual**: Pre-action check-in or ritual around what kinds of qualities your team wants to bring into the action, and what practices would support those qualities being experienced. Such as:

  o **Before an action**, singing, silence, creating an altar, or signing a nonviolence pledge

  o **During an action**, singing, silence, walking in a procession, creating an altar in the action space, agreeing to no signs or chants, incorporating art, the whole team dressing in a coherent and/or symbolic way.

- **Natural light**: We encourage teams to experiment with holding meetings and gatherings by natural light, sun by day and candlelight by night

Vocation

"May you find your passion and make it your gift
and your service, freely given with love."
~ Terry Tempest Williams ~

"When I dare to be powerful—to use my strength in
the service of my vision, then it becomes less and
less important whether I am afraid."
~ Audre Lorde ~

We understand "vocation" to be the gifts we are called to bring into the world and in direct action spaces. Living out our vocations within this network will strengthen and grow the broader movement ecosystem.

When we embody these gifts in service to disrupting systems of domination, our relationship to risk shifts. We are freed to show up more grounded in our own strength and in the clarity and power we establish together. We commit to dismantling barriers that stand in the way of individuals discovering, embracing, and living their purpose and taking action, especially those most impacted by these barriers.

When we embody our vocations in community, we are knitting together a particular kind of culture. This culture allows us to separate from ego and **find joy in the gifts** we bring forward together. In moments of decision about whose voice will be heard or who will lead in a particular way, an orientation toward vocation moves us to ask: "Whose gifts are a match for this context?" or "Which gifts are emerging from our team to meet this moment?"

It's important to remember that for a very long time the labor and gifts of women and BIPOC people have been extracted without compensation or consent. We work to build a community that supports people to give freely, from their own volition, with love. Additionally, we commit to supporting one another's vocational development, which includes a recognition that there are times in our lives when we are not free to offer our gifts or when it is not the right place or time to do so.

A practice of vocation pushes back against the narrative of the domination system that says "You must be everything for everyone." That false narrative is exhausting, manipulative, and does not allow us to fully **explore and experience our own power within**. This is often especially true within social change work and movement spaces, and limits the creative possibilities of what "direct action" can look like.

Most of us will embody multiple vocations, and sometimes we will struggle to discern what we are called to do or to be. When in doubt, we will encourage one another to experiment and see what happens. Each of us will make space and time for our teammates and others to bring their gifts forward.

> "Ask what makes you come alive, and go do it.
> Because what the world needs
> is people who have come alive"
>
> ~ Howard Thurman ~

Roles vs. vocations

Each of us will be called upon to step into a wide variety of roles in support of our teams, the broader network, and our partners and allies. We may do the dishes, give instruction to a group preparing for action, follow the leadership of others, or facilitate a particular meeting. The roles we choose to fill in support of the shared work do not necessarily define, amplify, or diminish our vocations.

Many people in our movement take on roles without a full and authentic sense of consent or joy. Probably, this is because many of these roles are assigned a certain value, or lack of value, by society at large. Our practice of vocation upends that paradigm. Our practice of vocation makes us more fully ourselves and more fully alive. To be fully alive is in direct opposition to a system of domination that requires us to make choices that make us feel dead inside in order to operate within it.

The work of building resilient communities of resistance and transformation requires that each of us take responsibility for a variety of tasks. Because our roles are often not expressive of our vocations, we **strive to remember: It is not our vocation to be smaller than we are, even though sometimes it is our role to be.** We will encourage one another to find a healthy balance between taking on roles that free others to bring their gifts and bringing our own gifts forward.

Since its inception, this network has dreamed of a transformed movement culture and transformed movement spaces, where a beautiful array of people who may never have considered themselves "activists" will bring their gifts and their full selves into the mix, and be welcomed and celebrated. Our hope is that the coming together of such a mix of vocations in movement spaces will unleash power and beauty we haven't yet seen.

Many of us have had the experience of being a newcomer to a movement organization or campaign, and being greeted with an explanation of what we need to do to get with the program. Our network wants to welcome a newcomer differently, asking with genuine curiosity: "Who are you? What gifts are yours to bring? How can we work together to activate your vocation as fully as possible as part of the network?"

What gifts are needed? Conflict transformers, musicians, artists, actors, educators, documenters, builders, dismantlers, strategists, everything-riskers, listeners, monastics and other deep pray-ers and presencers, medics and other healers, group process virtuosos, story-tellers, radio broadcasters, cooks, resource collectors and distributors, dumpster divers, clowns and jugglers. The list is endless.

An example of how vocation might be honored and uplifted by a team

A teammate whose vocation is to be a prankster might be great at idea genera-tion but terrible at putting those ideas on paper or evaluating their feasi-bility. Someone with the vocation of slowness and introspection may be the perfect person to add to the conversa-tion. This also frees the prankster up to say "I can't do this alone," which in and of itself is a powerful act.

Recommended practices

- **Personal discernment**: What is it that you feel most deeply called to contribute to this work? Spend up to an hour on your own being with/living into this question. This hour can incorporate music, meditation, journaling, walking in nature, whatever will best serve this type of introspection and discernment for you.

- **Vocation sharing circle**: Create an explicit time to share in rounds:

  o How you see your vocation, or what you are currently practicing on the journey to seeing it. Be sure to acknowledge the vulnerability inherent in asking yourself, as Mary Oliver encourages, "What is it you plan to do with your one wild and precious life?" This is important for a team without previous experience of working together closely, as well as for people who know each other deeply, but from a different context. Take notes on a large piece of paper about each person's vocation(s), and then look at the patterns. What does this reveal to you about the purpose and direction of your team?

Example: In their vocation sharing
circle, a new team learns that two of
their people have a vocational call
to singing and songwriting. Another is
called to ceremony and ritual, another
to healing and caregiving, and the
last has a gift for public-speaking
and pageantry. As they look together
at what might be possible for them as a
team purpose, a vision emerges of theat-
rical, ceremonial intervention within
halls of power.

- **Naming vocations in others:** Offer regular
"noticings" in relation to your teammates'
vocations. Offer acknowledgment and feedback about times when you have witnessed
your teammates standing in their vocations.
We do this because the mirror that community
can provide is a powerful aid to seeing our
own vocations. What this might look like:
"Wow, at the action last week I noticed your
careful attentiveness to the wellness of our
team. When Sandra was feeling overwhelmed, I
saw you attend to her needs with great care.
That is one of the indispensable gifts I see
you offering our team."

A more challenging form of "noticing"
to openly practice with one another is
lovingly speaking the truth when we see

others pursuing a path that doesn't actually reflect true giftedness. Sometimes our guesses at vocation point to what we wish were true about ourselves and our gifts, while not actually reflecting what's real. Faulty guesses at our vocation can trap us in roles, projects, training and/or other responsibilities that simply aren't a genuine fit for us, and sometimes such traps hold us for months or even years before we're able to admit to ourselves what's happening. This kind of "noticing" requires us to offer feedback skillfully, in a context of deep care and trust. This is a practice of fierce vulnerability for both the giver and receiver of such feedback. If done well it can help circumvent a lot of unhappiness and clear the way for true gifts yet to be revealed.

The hope here is that structured time offering such sharing about our vocations and our noticings about the vocations of others will make us more apt to offer such feedback informally on a regular basis. In this way we hope to build a vocation-oriented, vocation-positive culture.

- **Vocation partners**: Your vocation partner is someone who helps you to answer questions like: Do you feel your gifts are being honored and engaged by this team? How can I

support you to do what you came here
to do? Perhaps make time once a month to
have a conversation about vocation with
your partner.

- **"Whose gift is this to do?"**: Make it an
  intentional practice for your team in
  check-ins or in planning meetings to ask the
  question, "Whose gift is this to do?" Make
  it a part of your campaign planning documents. We all do better at stepping back
  when we have trust that our gifts are seen
  and valued, and that they will be called
  upon when needed.

Emergence

"What you can plan is too small for you to live."
~ David Whyte ~

Through direct observation of nature's patterns and systems, we see life's capacity to resolve incredibly complex problems and to thrive. Indigenous cultures the world over have cultivated and practiced ways of living on earth, on earth's terms.

We seek to embody this to the best of our abilities by re-learning how to align ourselves with ecological patterns, and by **reminding ourselves to *sense and respond* rather than *predict and control*.**

In the face of multiplying, intensifying crises, we do not know what will bring a life-affirming culture into being. **The mistaken belief that we can analyze, solve, and control seems only to speed the unraveling and is, in fact, part of the cycle of domination we are working to end and heal from.**

David Whyte's quote above reminds us that the nature of our future lies beyond our strategic plans or even our wildest dreams. Emergence calls us to put our faith in a path revealing itself that is not yet visible, or which might never become visible to one person alone. While recognizing the importance of developing goals and strategies, we emphasize just as strongly paying attention and listening for what needs to happen next. **Aligning with emergence does not exclude planning and strategy.** Emergence points us to adaptive strategy.

Perhaps you have been part of a direct action when, after a setback or a period of confusion, the energy plummets. Out of nowhere someone raises their voice in song. There is a shift in energy, and the tone of the action is transformed. This unplanned strategy was possible because one person was listening deeply, and sensed what was needed in that moment. From there, a song emerged.

Emergence is not a replacement for structure. Structure is the container that supports us to notice and respond as part of an effective living system.

Our intention is to build practices into our systems that amplify the voices that are least heard. Listening to the universe is usually not about hearing what is loudest or most immediate. The voice of each and every member of our network is invaluable and essential to our planning and strategizing.

```
Domination has defined effectiveness and
winning as results that can be measured
and made tangible. However, it is quite
likely we may never know the true impact
of our actions. Emergence calls us to
cultivate faith that the integrity of
our actions will contribute to the cause
of justice, whether or not we see the
immediate results we may be hoping for.
```

Coming back to earth

For many of us, the commitment to the whole of this work, and to learning from emergence specifically, is inextricably linked with **a profound longing to come back to earth**. We yearn for more and deeper connection with the natural world, and experience this yearning as inseparable from a feeling of immeasurable loss.

We recognize that our alienation from wild places and the wildness of our own bodies and spirits is both the cause and the outcome of this current age of unraveling. We mourn our domestication as subjects of the domination system, and we have a longing beyond words for liberation and return.

> "The grief and sense of loss, that we often interpret as a failure in our personality, is actually a feeling of emptiness where a beautiful and strange otherness should have been encountered."
> ~ Paul Shepard ~

In the not-too-distant past, our ancestors did not see themselves as separate from our non-human kin and living habitats. We are determined to bridge the gap between our current lives and the lives lived by those ancestors, who understood our deeper connection. Entrusting ourselves to emergence, we enter the sacredness of listening and responding to the earth and to the parts of ourselves that remain untouched by domination and separation. In doing so we trust that whatever actions we choose to take will be creative, soulful, and mysterious in ways we would never otherwise discover.

Decentralized and self-organizing

Emergence inspires us to be a **decentralized** and **self-organizing network**. A team does not have to wait to get approval from another group to organize an action. As a given situation unfolds, our network will have the advantage of rapid response based on what is emerging in the moment, whereas most structures of the extractive economy depend on feeding information and decisions through a centralized chain of command.

In situations that do not call for such rapid response, decentralization creates space for **many minds to generate solutions** to problems and to quickly learn from each other what works and what doesn't. By experimenting with many different solutions, the learning of the whole often happens more quickly, and solutions emerge that could never have been dreamt up by a centralized structure.

All of this points toward the dispersed iterative design of our network. Meaning, the network will take shape based on innovations that build on one another, made by the people who are closest to particular problems and opportunities. We are gradually building small and scalable solutions that adapt to each circumstance based on the feedback that is being received.

Our society is unraveling. Conventional structures of organizing (corporations, nonprofits, typical systems of governance) are increasingly fragile and ill-equipped to respond to the world as it is. It's time to experiment with structures that get stronger with change instead of falling apart. **Healthy decentralized and self-organizing structures are strong enough to activate beautiful and powerful work, while remaining nimble enough to innovate and transform amidst great upheaval.**

Recommended practices

- **Silence**: In addition to the network's centering practice at the beginning of team meetings (see the "sample agenda" in the Decision-Making section), schedule other times for shared silence and meditation, and intersperse silence whenever it can help to ground the group and its process. Members are encouraged to do the same on an individual basis as well.

- **Earth relationship**: At network gatherings, incorporate shared practices for connecting with the earth and the more-than-human world: such as, finding a spot outdoors to regularly return to and spend time (sometimes called a "sit spot"), gardening, long walks in the woods, stargazing sessions.

- **Multi-day experiences out with the land**: Solo or team retreats and/or adventures in wild places, to observe, learn from, and delight in the workings of the natural world, and to hone our emergence listening skills.

- **Host the *"Council of All Beings"***: "[...]a communal ritual in which participants step aside from their human identity and speak on behalf of another life-form. A simple structure for spontaneous expression, it aims to heighten awareness of our interdependence in the living body of

Earth, and to strengthen our commitment to defend it." For more information on this powerful process designed by Joanna Macy, see https://bit.ly/3xg-SLes.

- **Technology awareness**: Reflect on your personal relationship to technology use and make specific personal commitments to reduce engagement with and dependence on tech devices and tech-heavy habits (i.e., discontinuing social media, limiting computer use and/or screen time of any kind to certain days or times, getting rid of certain devices altogether). This is a powerful complement to the network's commitment to tech-free meeting/ gathering spaces.

- **Unplugging/candlelight practice**: Spend entire stretches of time (an evening, a weekend, a week, a month, etc.) without the use of electricity, including electric lights. Try having a team meeting by candlelight, and notice how it impacts your team's field.

- **Talking circles**: Hold regular talking circles to share stories, build and strengthen relationships and practice deep listening.

- **Empty chair**: During team meetings and network gatherings leave an empty chair to represent those not present or without voice in the human and more-than-human world.

As long as we insist on relating to it strictly on on our own terms - as strange to us or subject to us - the wilderness is alien, threatening, fearful. We have no choice then but to become its exploiters,

and to lose, by consequence,

our place in it.

-Wendell Berry

NETWORK STRUCTURE

Basic Structure, Membership, and Onboarding

"Critical connections must precede critical mass."

~ adrienne maree brown ~

(inspired by Grace Lee Boggs)

Important Reminder

Until the network has an official onboarding process in place, please keep in mind that:

o References to the onboarding process should be translated by the reader as *the onboarding process still* being developed.

o References to members and teams should be translated as *unofficial members* and *unofficial teams*.

In lieu of an onboarding process, we encourage prospective members of the network to organize themselves into unofficial teams, using this handbook as their guide.

While some of the content in this section is aspirational, the descriptions and structures included here will serve as helpful guard rails for unofficial teams as they experiment with the network's principles and practices. This section also provides essential information for those developing and experimenting with training models that we trust will eventually evolve into the network's official onboarding process.[19]

At its core, FVN is a network of decentralized teams of 3-8ish people engaged in our movement DNA—its principles and practices. However, we are also deeply aware that we cannot exist as a network without a wider ecosystem within which teams operate. Below is a brief sketch of our network's structure, and the different ways in which one can be in relationship with it.

The Wider Movement Ecosystem

From its inception, our network has seen itself as one ingredient within a vast and complex recipe. We are not here to tell others how to do things, or to convince others to join us unless it's a genuinely snug fit. We're here because we want to bring our offering into the greater mix of the larger movement ecosystem.

---

19. Visit thefvn.org to stay updated on the status of our development of the onboarding process and national structure for the network.

Tackling white supremacy and the climate emergency is a massive undertaking, and we won't be able to do much of anything if we are acting in isolation. The broad spectrum of activist groups, coalitions, faith communities, organizations, and campaigns that make up the movement ecosystem is utterly essential to this undertaking. We are all in this together.

> During the founding of All of Us or None (AOUON), the country's first network of formerly incarcerated organizers, co-founder Dorsey Nunn explained that AOUON was a movement, not an organization. He went on to say that he hoped members of this new movement wouldn't take off their organization's hat and replace it with an AOUON hat. Instead, he encouraged people to keep their organization's hat on, and to put an AOUON pin onto that hat. This is a great analogy for our network's commitment to cross-fertilization and coalition-building.

It follows that we want to blur the line between whether someone is a part of "our network" or "that other organization." We are committed to fostering a network culture that provides nourishment to the larger ecosystem of movements. We, therefore, don't compete with other groups or "poach" their members.

In fact, we celebrate FVN teams that exist within the boundaries of other organizations. If members of Climate Justice Group X are inspired by our network's DNA, there is not a need for them to leave Climate Justice Group X to join FVN. Rather, they can consider starting an FVN team within Climate Justice Group X's boundaries.

Network Communities

Many people are inspired by the network and want to be involved but for any number of reasons aren't ready or don't wish to be part of a team. **We acknowledge this network isn't a small commitment**. We celebrate discernment about what relationship will best serve each person's life.

Each team in our network belongs to a larger network community made up of folks in the team's area who resonate with the network's principles and practices. These are people who participate in the work and life of the network, but who have not joined a team or collective.

There are innumerable ways to be engaged. For example, some people may participate in network events, trainings, and public actions. Some may be key partners in direct action campaigns. A masseuse might offer free massages in their network community. A therapist might gift therapy. Others might do the reparations self-audit and begin a personal reparations practice. Another person might offer free or affordable housing to a team member. Yet another might host network gatherings at their home or place of work. Others might develop an earth-connection practice or buddy up with someone to practice giving and receiving feedback.

In Buddhism, a large community of lay people are critical in supporting monastics (monks and nuns) and their ability to focus on their spiritual path. Lay people are not "less" Buddhist than the monastics, nor are they less committed to the path of liberation. They play a different role, and both monastic and lay communities are a necessary part of the Buddhist ecosystem.

Some people in the network community may eventually feel led to join or form a team. Others will continue to contribute in other ways that don't include team membership. Every community contribution is a gift to the network, and it is our hope that the presence of network teams will be a gift to their communities. Our teams would be hard-pressed to do what they're called to do without the love, support, and companionship of the network community that they co-create.

Members

As soon as our network's onboarding process is in place, anyone who feels called to uphold the network's shared principles and practices will be welcome to enter that process in order to become a member of the network.

A person's membership will be ongoing as long as they uphold the network's principles and practices within the context of an active team.

Teams

The purpose of a team is for its members to form a **home of mutual support, co-creativity, accountability, and action**. Teams engage in the network's **core and recommended practices** in order to foster self and collective transformation and to strengthen trust and skills for direct action, reparations, and the many facets of self-organizing.

A team is composed of **3+ people** who choose to become a team and have successfully completed the network's onboarding process. **It is recommended that teams with more than eight members split into two teams**. Generally speaking, the larger a group gets the harder it is to maintain strong working relationships and to make decisions together. For our network specifically, eight has been shown to be a healthy maximum for the decision-making process and meeting format our teams and collectives use.

For several reasons we recommend that new members form locally-based teams:

- Close proximity enables us to be together in-person more often, which supports the depth of relationship-building we're striving for.

- It's far easier for locally-based teams to take action together on an ongoing, consistent basis.

- Local teams share a local context, which strengthens a team's ability to dig in and follow through on locally-based campaigns, and to nurture meaningful long term, place-based movement relationships.

- Local teams are less dependent on carbon-heavy systems such as flying and driving long distances in order to meet and take action together.

Some teams will be more spread out than others. Each team is entrusted, therefore, to determine how far apart is too far apart for its prospective teammates, to set up a container that enables the team to uphold the network's principles and practices, and to thrive while doing so.

While most teams in the network will display a wide range of vocations, some teams might choose to join together around a specific one. For example, a group of musicians and street theater performers may choose to form a team, or a group that shares gift-edness in the healing arts or with documentation (through writing, photography, film or radio). Another team may be made up of members who belong to a faith community or grassroots organization.

Forming a team

- Ideally, prospective teams will go through the onboarding process together, but this isn't necessary. A team can be formed by any three or more people who have completed the onboarding process and who want to choose each other as teammates.

- Fewer than three onboarded people is considered a "team-in-formation" (because it is not yet a full team). We need webs of strong relationships to do this work. There is a big difference between the capacity of two people and the capacity of three people to support each other in the challenges we're taking on.

- Becoming a team with people is choosing to engage in deep work together. Teams are meant to become for each other a family with enough trust to take serious risks together.

Rather than choosing people based on their skill sets, first notice how you feel when you are with each other, and how you might be able to deepen your relationships—especially while moving through the challenging work of unmasking the violence of the status quo in the world around you and in yourselves.

- Be self-aware and resist the temptation to create cultures of sameness. Members of the network are encouraged to move beyond conventional social strategies for grouping. Consider yourself up to the challenge of valuing people for more than the type of clothing they wear or the age they are or the thing they just said. Dig deeper.

- If you haven't formed your team yet, start engaging with the network in whatever ways fit for you.[20] Cultivate relationships with other changemakers. Map your community and movement ecosystem to help determine where and how you might find your future teammates. Invite friends and allies to network events.

- Other teams can also support you to form your team. Is there anyone outside the

---

20. Visit thefvn.org for suggestions on how to get involved.

network who knows you well and can help you develop your team? Consider asking them for support.

- It is essential that each team is connected with other groups in the movement ecosystem, with other teams, former teammates after a team splits, etc. Consider and build these relationships continuously as part of your team formation.

Pollinators and pollinator teams

In our network, people who are not based in one location, or who hit the road often in service to the movement, are called "pollinators." These folks serve an important role in transferring practices, experiences, skills, learning, and care between teams.

Members who are pollinators are also part of teams. Each pollinator should have and maintain a strong connection with their teammates and spend significant time each year in the same place with their team. As with any other network member, pollinators uphold the network's principles and practices with their team.

While locally-based teams are standard for our network, a group of pollinators who have worked together for a long time and created deep trust may also choose to be a team together. An example of this is the Climate Disobedience Center (CDC), a pollinator team that is vocationally connected through their practice of direct action and their experience of direct action campaigns. Members of this team live in different locations but are committed to network principles and practices as a team.

Pollinator teams show up for direct action in the same place, but will likely hold their regular team meetings remotely. Because face-to-face time in addition to action days will be critical for team cohesion and relationship-building, pollinator teams are encouraged to build it in when they establish their rhythm of meetings.

Team size

As discussed previously, when your team gets to a size where it becomes hard to maintain a high level of trust and make decisions, we suggest splitting into two teams. This is a moment of joy and celebration that defies a deeply ingrained, growth-at-all-costs style of organizing. Our network's decision-making process and meeting format invites all voices. In order to balance this commitment to equity with our desire for efficiency, we recommend eight as a maximum for teams. Ultimately this decision is left to the discretion of each team. If a team with more than eight people is doing amazing work together and maintaining a high level of trust, by all means they are free to continue without splitting.

Some simple questions to help your team determine if it's time to split:

- Are we fulfilling our network commitments?
- How is communication going?
- Is there time and space to hear everyone's voices?
- Are we experiencing more conflict than we can adequately handle?
- Is everyone on the team engaged in the work and with one another?
- Are we having fun?

While splitting carries a negative connotation in many instances, in self-organizing it is a sign of growth and new life.

The splitting of a team is a transition that doesn't need to be viewed as an ending. The two teams resulting from a split can by all means continue to work together closely, and may even decide to meet and/or take action together on a regular basis.

Alongside the sadness that may come with the transition, a splitting team is encouraged to remember the reasons behind the split—smaller teams help bring about deeper trust, more agile decision-making, and more effective support in direct action. The process of determining the composition of the two new teams can also be used as an opportunity to reflect on affinity and the personal vocations present.

This is a moment to celebrate—our network is growing and adapting!

Leaving/dissolving a team

Members may choose to leave a team for many reasons including big life changes or shifting priorities. If any member chooses to leave a team, we encourage the person leaving the team to convey this decision in person, and for teams to organize a special circle process to honor the person leaving the team.

There may also be instances when it is time for an entire team to dissolve. In this case, we encourage you to come together for a closing ritual to honor each person and to honor the work you have done collectively. It is important to make the decision to dissolve your team transparent to your wider network community.

In either of the above cases, the following options are available for the individual(s):

1. Join a different team.

2. Start a new team.

3. Join the broader network community, and do 1 or 2 from above before two years pass. As the onboarding process is expected to evolve, if a member is inactive for two years or more, they are asked to go through the onboarding process again. If a person leaves a team then later chooses to rejoin the same team, a reintegration circle that gives voice to the feelings and needs of everyone involved is highly recommended. In like manner, if the person ends up joining a different pre-existing team, a welcome circle is highly recommended.

4. If a team member chooses to leave due to interpersonal conflicts or disagreements that remain unresolved after going through the network's conflict engagement process (see Restorative Conflict Engagement section), whenever possible teams should hold a circle (or create an alternative means for deep listening), so the departing member feels heard and any concerns that were not shared during the conflict engagement process can be gathered.

Teams are encouraged to report back to that person at a later time on how their concerns were integrated by the team.

Similarly, if a team decides to disband due to unresolved conflicts or disagreements, it is recommended that a circle is held where each member can speak their truth without feedback or cross talk. We recommend that this circle be held with a skilled third party facilitator.

5. If a person is leaving due to health, family matters, time scarcity (factors beyond the functions of a team), it is recommended that the team make every effort to determine if the team itself or the wider network community can address their needs and help them stay active.

Dissolution of membership

For information about the dissolution of membership see the Restorative Conflict Engagement section.

Key reflection questions and tips for teams

For many of us, **our lives will need to look very different** in order for us to take the risk of putting ourselves in the way of violent systems. What do we need to make this possible?

- Your team's home community is where the work of **community uplift** happens. What pieces of a new world are you most excited to build in your home community? Who should your team connect with to make this happen? Who is doing this work already?

- **Look around at other examples** of people who are replacing isolation with community, who are replacing lives based around life-taking resources with life-giving resources. Experiencing village is more powerful than explanation. Examples include: worker collectives, land trusts, community farms, cooperative houses, eco-villages, Catholic Worker communities, and mutual aid projects.

- The **relational** is essential. We seek to build and nurture real, meaningful connections.

- These connections are **strategic**. Let's build connections that make everyone's work more effective. No team can hold all the skills, perspectives, and experiences needed. Many of the gaps in our teams can be strengthened through our community connections.

- When your team is preparing to enter **direct action**, consider what support you will need (logistical, strategic, legal, emotional). How are you setting yourselves up to get help from your network community so you can enter into action spaces with abundant resources to share rather than taking more resources than you offer? How can you prepare so that taking action is not debilitating for your home community, so people feel more connected and supported rather than drained?

- Collaborate with **other teams in the network**!

- Collaborate with **groups outside the network**!

- **Network trainings** and other trainings in your community are a great way to connect with other people. Join with other groups to bring in people with more experience and learn together.

- Early gatherings during the initial stages of the network included **open houses** so each person's home community could learn

about what these loved ones were up to. We
encourage teams to host such gatherings
regularly.

Collectives

When network members discover that something important is
missing in the network, or that something beautiful can be added,
they are encouraged to take the initiative, self-organize, and offer a
gift to the network community in the form of a network collective.

Over the course of our network's journey, we expect that
members will self-organize to establish a wide spectrum of such
collectives. They could look like so many vocations: grief tending,
song keeping, art building, campaign consulting, medic support.
Or they may organize around a certain identity or shared practice.
There may be a BIPOC-only collective and an elder's collective, for
example. There may be a meditation and prayer collective and a vegan
collective.

Some collectives may last for a short period—for the duration of a particular campaign or however long it takes to organize a
regional gathering of some kind, for example. Other collectives will
be ongoing.

Key attributes of network collectives:

- Any member can form a collective if they see
  the need for a group of people across teams
  to address something relevant to our shared
  work.

- Network members initiate and populate the collectives.

- These members may choose to invite non-members, such as mentors and experts, to participate as consultants to the collective, but they will not be decision-making members of the collective.

- Network collectives uphold the network's DNA and utilize its five operational systems.

- Because they are task-specific, collectives are especially encouraged to pay close attention to the vocational gifts and aspirations of those who wish to participate, and those who ought to be invited to participate because they are a great vocational fit for the work at hand.

- The foundational unit of a collective is organized as a decision-making circle. Because collectives use the network's decision-making process and meeting format, eight members is strongly recommended as a maximum for a collective's main circle of decision-makers.

- Depending on the nature of a collective's work, it may organize itself into multiple circles. For example, a collective may have a main decision-making circle and additional

sub-circles to carry out various aspects of
the collective's work. Generally speaking,
at the sub-circle level collectives are
encouraged to keep numbers small (2-4) for
the sake of efficient workflow and communication.

An aspirational national collective structure

The following core collectives are central components of a national
structure envisioned during the DNA-building process, but not yet
seen through to implementation.

- **Power and Access**: Holding the complexities of how power and privilege show up in
  diverse organizing spaces and supporting
  our ongoing commitments to equity and to
  fostering and taking leadership from people
  from marginalized communities.

- **Onboarding**: Developing and implementing
  the network's onboarding process, including
  developing curriculum and training trainers.

- **Conflict Engagement**: Supporting network
  members in developing their skills for
  healthy conflict engagement, as well as
  direct support in navigating conflicts that
  are not able to be managed internally within
  or between teams.

- **Coaching**: Supporting members and teams, particularly new ones, in deepening their understanding and practice of the network DNA.

- **Network Feedback**: Receiving feedback about what is and is not working within the network and finding ways to integrate those lessons back into the system.

- **Internal Reparations**: Facilitating the flow of reparations within the network.

- **DNA Revision**: Reviewing the feedback received by the Network Feedback Collective during the network's soft launch and incorporating it into an updated version of the handbook.

- **Stewardship Circle**: Serving as the hub for information sharing and cross-fertilization between the network's Core Collectives.

At the time of this writing, we have determined that the network does not yet have the capacity to bring this envisioned national structure to life. We have included a sketch of it in the Appendices, however, including detailed descriptions of the above collectives. Our hope is that these resources will inform the efforts of future network members and teams as they determine which structures will best serve the network as it evolves.

In the meantime, we urge each network community and team to think about the roles that each of the above Core Collectives are meant to serve, and attempt to fulfill these roles as much as possible at the local level.

Nationwide Localism

Every member in our network commits to upholding our shared principles and practices, and, ultimately, every member determines the particular way they will apply them. We are a network of autonomous teams responding to specific needs in our own communities and regions.

Whenever necessary, any and every team is free to put the call out across the network for collective mobilization.

How To Join the Network

Until the network has an official onboarding process in place, we encourage those who feel called to uphold the network's shared principles and practices to organize themselves into unofficial teams, using this handbook as their guide. Visit thefvn.org to stay updated on the status of our development of the onboarding process, and to connect with others who have organized or who wish to organize unofficial teams. During the network's soft launch, the flow of mutual support and learning between teams is absolutely essential.

The Onboarding Process
Still Being Developed

While prospective network members are familiarizing themselves with this handbook—some of whom will also organize themselves into unofficial teams—we encourage different regions across the country to develop models of an onboarding process. In following our commitments to decentralization and emergence, we hope and trust that these varied experiments—based on the cultures, needs, and capacities of the different regions—will give us critical feedback about what works, what doesn't, and what our needs are moving forward.

Because of the depth of work we hope to do within our network, we envision that the onboarding process will be a deep time-intensive experience or set of experiences that will:

1. Introduce prospective members to the ethos of fierce vulnerability;
2. Deepen prospective members' understanding of the network's entire DNA, including its systems and structure, as described in this handbook;
3. Give prospective members ample opportunity to begin practicing the DNA; and,
4. Include an intentional discernment process to ensure this network is a good fit for them.

Post-onboarding—or perhaps it will be seen as an open-ended continuation of the onboarding process—we also envision that members will participate in ongoing training to support continued learning and growth.

As regions engage in their onboarding experiments, we request that the lessons learned be fed back into the network ecosystem, where they can be synthesized and a national onboarding process can eventually be agreed upon. At that point our soft launch will transition into a full-fledged launch, and both unofficial members and newcomers to the network will have the opportunity to onboard as FVN's first cohort of official members.

We will attempt to do everything we can to make this process as accessible as possible to those who are interested in it, including making resources available to BIPOC participants through our internal reparations fund.

Walk
as if
you

are
kissing
the
earth
with
your
feet

Thich
Nhat
Hanh

OUR LIVING SYSTEMS

Principles of Self-Organizing

Our network invites emergence by embracing key principles of self-organizing, drawn from the wisdom of living systems:

- We are a decentralized living system made up of a web of relationships. We hold relational health and trust-building as primary.

- We are a learning system, evolving constantly.

- We endeavor to stay clear about our identity and purpose, while remaining flexible and adaptable.

- We seek the mysterious paradoxical combination of full personal autonomy and deep collective unity.

- We listen deeply to and are shaped by those targeted by colonization, white supremacy, patriarchy, and other interconnected systems of oppression.

- We seek to make all information within our system available to everyone. Nothing is hidden or hoarded for power.

- What we do and how we do it are most meaningful to us, not the eloquence of our written materials or our professed values.

- We invite our members' whole selves into the system and do our best to show up authentically.

- We are willing to experiment, and to make, learn from, and repair the impacts of our mistakes.

- No one member or subset of members speaks for the network. All members do.

Five Operational Systems

A common misconception about decentralized groups and organizations is that they are structureless. On the contrary, healthy decentralization depends largely on robust, replicable structures and systems—oftentimes more than hierarchical groups employ.

In order to support our network's particular aims, we give especially careful attention to five operational systems, adapted from the work of Miki Kashtan and the Nonviolent Global Liberation community:

Decision-making
Resource Flow
Information Flow
Giving and Receiving Feedback
Restorative Conflict Engagement

Whether or not we openly acknowledge them, there will be some way in which we handle these five essential functions. When these functions are not co-held within a set of agreements supporting equity and belonging, groups usually default to patriarchal patterns inherited from the dominant culture. For this reason we approach these five systems deliberately, with clear intentions rooted in our shared principles and values.

The network's five systems are described in the sections to follow.

Decision-making: how we determine a way forward

Clear decision-making structure is key to liberatory work. Recognizing the emotional need to be seen, heard, and valued during a process of making decisions is critical. In doing so, we also need to be aware of how the traditional pooling of power along lines of privilege can create inequity in decision-making.

Network teams and collectives share a common decision-making process and meeting format that supports efficiency and equitable participation. Drawing on training, research and experience with Sociocracy and the Advice Process we have identified a set of principles and practices for group meetings and group decision-making that reflects our values, and we ask all teams and collectives to adopt them as a baseline framework. This is an essential way for us to collectively counteract patriarchal conditioning.

Without a commitment to a power-equalizing alternative, groups almost always revert to the default meeting and decision-making habits instilled by our patriarchal domination system, which reinforce the prioritization of certain voices and certain concerns over others.

Our network's meeting format and consent-based decision-making process will be key elements of our future onboarding process. In the meantime, to learn these forms we recommend that unofficial teams connect with Sociocracy for All—an excellent training resource for all things related to Sociocracy.[21]

After a team has gained some mastery of consent-based decision-making and the sociocratic meeting format, they are encouraged to experiment with these forms and make adjustments to make them their own. It is both important for our network to share this common framework, and for teams to utilize it in a way that feels true to their varying personalities, cultures and needs.

Needs, principles, and tools[22]

In our meetings and decision-making processes we seek:

Belonging

Learning

Mattering

Choice

Connection

Efficiency

Agency

Clarity

We follow several guiding principles as we meet and make decisions together, including:

"Safe enough to try"

"Good enough for now"

---

21. You can also reach out to FVN (`thefvn.org`) for an update on network training opportunities related to decision-making and meeting format.

22. These lists of needs, principles, and essential tools draw heavily from Sociocracy for All (`sociocracyforall.org`).

"I can work with this"[23]
Distributed leadership
Seek the win-win
A feedback rich environment
Openness to emergence
Transparency
No one ignored

Some of the essential meeting and decision-making tools we use:

Rounds (go-arounds where everyone has a voice)
Check-Ins/Check-outs
Tension Checks
Clarity and consistency of roles
Advice Process
Meeting evaluations

Sample agenda

The following sample agenda of a team (or collective) meeting illustrates the basic elements of the network's basic meeting format. Additional practices can be added before, after, or within this meeting format, such as several of the recommended practices included in the previous Core Commitments sections. While this format won't necessarily apply to all team meetings (i.e., quarterly reflection circles or other relational or content-specific meetings may benefit from a different container), it provides a shared baseline for regular meetings for planning, information-sharing and decision-making.

---

23. As opposed to pushing for personal preference.

Centering practice	e.g. 3-10 minutes of shared silence, body scan, song, reading of a poem, prayer, or short passage.	Purpose: spiritual grounding, embodiment
Check-in round	Each person shares how they are as they show up for the meeting, and anything that feels important to share in order to feel present in the meeting space.	Purpose: Self-connection, heart-connection with others
Tension check	Also in the form of a round, where each person is asked to name any present tensions in themselves or in the group that might somehow get in the way or otherwise impact the group as they proceed with the meeting.	Purpose: Surfacing conflict is essential to group togetherness (which ultimately enables things to get done)
Agenda review and consent round	Round for suggested adjustments, round for consent to agenda.	Purpose: transparency, efficiency

Content items	We use Sociocratic tools and processes for a full spectrum of such content.	Purpose: To move the work forward with intention, clarity and efficiency
These could be any number of things: • reports • a pre-prepared proposal to be explored and decided on using consent process • picture-forming to shape a new proposal or action plan • getting the group's feedback about something • evaluating some piece of work that's been done • a selection process for a new role		
Quick meeting evaluation	A round to hear what worked well, what didn't work well, and ideas about improving things in the next meeting.	Purpose: Feedback, learning and growth
Check-out round	Each person shares how they're feeling here at the end of the meeting.	Purpose: to provide a sense of closure and togetherness

Three basic meeting roles for teams and collectives

We recommend that these three roles are covered. Teams and collectives may decide whether they wish to circulate roles among their members or to establish set terms.

The **Coordinator** is responsible for:

- Making sure meeting dates, times, and locations (virtual meeting information, as the case may be) are set, and communicated to all members well in advance of meetings

- Requesting agenda items and suggestions from members

- Working with facilitator to prepare working agendas in advance of meetings

- Sending reminders to members a day or two before meetings, inclusive of the proposed agenda and any other pertinent information

The **Facilitator** is responsible for:

- Working with coordinator to prepare working agendas in advance of meetings

- Facilitating meetings using our sociocracy-inspired meeting format and decision-making process

The **Note-taker** is responsible for:

- Taking notes for all meetings, capturing key considerations, decisions, and action items

- Organizing all meeting notes in a running archive (digital or hard copy)

- Making meeting notes available to any member upon request

Tech-free meeting spaces

In support of connection, belonging, and creating a field conducive to heart-centered work, teams are asked to hold network gatherings and meetings of all kinds (training, planning, visioning, decision-making, debriefing, fun and fellowship) tech free. Network members and other participants from the network community are asked to not bring phones, computers, and other tech gadgets into the meeting/gathering space, and notes are taken by hand.[24]

Exceptions may be made at the discretion of those in attendance. Possible reasons for this exception might include: a physical disability that makes some form of high tech necessary, placing a call to someone outside of the space in order that they might join the conversation; using the internet or a computer for some specific research or training purpose that is of significant relevance to the

---

24. Teams and collectives are encouraged to adapt this as necessary during the COVID-19 pandemic, while attempting to stay true to this practice as much as possible.

meeting. When a device is used for such a purpose, participants are encouraged to treat it as analogous to pulling a book off a bookshelf in order to get a particular piece of information, after which the book (the device) is returned to the shelf. In some contexts, a team may determine that meeting via phone or video call, though not ideal, is their best option. Some examples include: using phone or video calls to host pollinator team meetings between the times when the team can be physically together; using technology to enable safe team meetings and connection to continue during a global pandemic.

Depending on the physical space it may be helpful to identify a tech zone, where devices can be stored. You may also wish to structure specific times for folks to engage with their tech.

Advice Process

While our network does not use the Advice Process as our baseline decision-making framework, it is an extremely valuable complement to our Sociocracy-informed decision-making system.

In a nutshell, according to Frederic Laloux's description in *Reinventing Organizations*, the Advice Process says that any member can make any decision after seeking advice from 1) everyone who will be meaningfully affected by the decision and 2) people with expertise on the matter. Following Miki Kashtan's recommendation (which is not included in Laloux's Advice Process description), in our own experiments with this process, we've also experienced the value of seeking advice from 3) people who have the resources needed to implement decisions, and therefore the ability to undermine the decision in question (such as people with a significant amount of power in the system). Advice received must be taken into consideration. The point is not to create a watered-down compromise that accommodates everybody's wishes. It is about accessing collective wisdom in pursuit of a sound decision. With all the advice and perspectives the decision-maker has received, they choose what they believe to be the best course of action.

Steps in the Advice Process:

1. Someone notices a problem or opportunity and takes the initiative, or alerts someone better positioned to do so.

2. The decision-maker seeks input to sound out perspectives before proposing action.

3. The decision-maker crafts a proposal and seeks advice about it from those affected, those with expertise, and possibly those uniquely positioned to undermine the decision.

4. Taking this advice into account, the decision-maker decides on an action and informs those who have given advice.

In our network, it is not the case that any member can make any decision after seeking advice along the lines described above. But we do enthusiastically encourage network members to use the Advice Process and to move forward with decisions about matters that prove non-controversial through the process. This allows everyone in the network to seize the initiative on a great many things, and very help-fully reduces the amount of decisions that need to be made in group meetings.

We also encourage and celebrate members using steps 1, 2, and 3 above in order to craft proposals informally outside of team meetings. Such proposals have a great chance of receiving the consent of the group, because they have already been vetted and likely helpfully revised over the course of the process.

Resource flow: how we deal with money

One of the ways racial and climate injustice are most deeply coded into our society is through a system of economics that sees Black, brown, Indigenous, non-male bodies and our Earth as stores to be extracted from and sewers to be discarded into. This system fosters a winner-loser mentality that prizes individual accumulation and hoarding over reciprocity and community. This worldview impacts most every aspect of our lives.

No matter how much we long for a different world, our work in this network will require some interaction with this economic system, including directing the energy of money toward our shared goals. Given this inevitability, our practice is to be fiercely vulnerable in relationship with one another, so that we can build flows of financial resources that begin to heal rather than exacerbate inequity.

One way to articulate our aspiration with regard to resource flow is that we wish to practice a "relational" rather than "transactional" economy. In a relational economy, the core principle is that resources flow from where they are to where they are needed. This is demonstrated in all natural systems, through the cycling of nutrients, energy, and water. Human beings have blocked this flow through the idea of a separate self that should exchange, own, and accumulate resources. Our work is to undo the ideas of "deserve" and "mine" to allow this natural flow to resume.

When a community practices relational economics, each member shares both resources and risks. We have developed practices (described below) to share resources and aspire toward shared risks.

One way to understand sharing resources and risk is "As long as I have food, you will not be hungry," or "As long as I am alive, your children will be cared for." We believe that this level of commitment to one another is worth aspiring to and that it will enable us to take the sort of action we feel called to take at this moment in history.

> See "Principles of Gift Economics" in the Appendices for a helpful description of the foundational values of the gift economy: Generosity, Access, Interdependence, Intentionality, Equity, Transparency, and Faith.
>
> Five key features of the Gift Economy[25] that flow from those values are:
> 1) No price, No fee
> 2) Voluntary Giving to "Pay It Forward"
> 3) Giving in Response to Need
> 4) Giving in Proportion to One's Ability
> 5) Information & Feedback Flow Freely

25. These five features were originally articulated by the East Bay Meditation Center (EBMC). See https://bit.ly/3705siK for more on EBMC's generosity-based "All-Dana" model.

Practicing relational economics

We work to operate in the relational economy, rather than the exchange economy, wherever possible. This includes how we resource the normal course of our work together as teams, as well as when we take action, plan a retreat, or attend a gathering.

Sample relational economics questions to help identify resources to support an event:

- Who do we know who might find great joy in hosting our meeting in their living room?

- Who has a spare bedroom or floor space that could host our members that are coming in from elsewhere?

- Who do we know who would love to cook for this group?

- Who has access to food they would be excited to share or offer? This might be from their garden, their workplace, or another source they know of.

- Who do we know who might enjoy the opportunity to connect through picking someone up from the train station?

Sample questions to support the practice of relational economics within a team:

- Who has the knowledge or skill we are needing and would find joy in teaching us?

- Who can fix the door that has fallen off its hinges in my house?

- Does anyone have an old computer I can use?

- Would someone be able to pick my daughter up from school so I can attend our meetings?

In this way we avoid renting spaces, staying at hotels, hiring people, ordering pizza, taking taxis, and other ways that capitalism has trained us to meet our needs through transactions.

This meets two goals:

1. We knit the social fabric of our network more snugly, building power through deepening relationships and meeting everyone's need to contribute and be needed by others.

2. We reduce the amount of financial resources needed to do our work, making participation accessible to more people.

Internal and external reparations

We recognize and acknowledge that the flow of financial resources in our society has been and still is violently shaped by white supremacy, patriarchy and colonization. We actively work to repair this through directing the flow of resources toward network members and other communities that have been and are still being extracted from. Please see the Reparations section for specific network practices around both internal and external reparations. Additional practices follow below.

Where money lives and how it moves

Each team should engage in a decision-making process to choose where to keep financial resources in a way that works for everyone involved. Be careful to understand the tax implications of where your resources are held. It might be that you keep resources in one of your personal bank accounts, or it might be that you keep everything in cash in a box, or that your team opens a bank account or Paypal account. It might be that an existing non-profit or organization connected to your team is willing to house your financial resources. Whatever you decide, make sure that everyone understands the choice that was made, and that there is a clear plan for how to ensure the money is used for the purposes for which it is intended.

Your team's flow of resources may include providing financial resources to folks for their time in order for them to be able to participate in the network. You will want to consider the tax implications of this. Maybe they are set up as a contractor to a non-profit or organization that is holding the funds. Maybe they are paid in cash from money collected at events or gatherings. Be sure that you have a plan for how this will happen before you promise funds to anyone, so that it can happen in a timely, consensual way. If it is more than a one-time payment, you may wish to write up a shared agreement so that everyone involved knows how and when money will move.

Sharing costs for events

Whenever we organize an action, workshop or gathering in the name of the network, we work to make visible and collectivize the financial costs of putting it on. Transparency is a core value.

For each event, teams should designate one or two people to be responsible for the financial resources for the event, known as the "Money Stewards." The Money Stewards are responsible for ensuring that anyone on the team or collective can access the information of what money is coming in, from whom, and what money is going out, to whom and for what purpose.

Money Stewards can use this spreadsheet or something similar to track income and expenses: `https://bit.ly/36bdCBc`.

People and teams within the network have experimented with different models of how to make visible and collectivize costs for an event that incorporates our commitment to the Gift Economy. There is no one "right way" to be in the Gift Economy. We encourage each team to experiment with a model that works for them that is explicit and is grounded in shared values. Below is the basic framework shared amongst the various models we have experimented with.

Step One: When people are new to the network or to our resource flow practices, in advance of the event, inform all participants that this gathering is happening with a Gift Economics framework, and that there will be an opportunity to give resources to support the needs of the organizers and the costs of the event as well as for participants to request resources to support their needs in attending the event.

Step Two: Transparency and naming your needs is key in the Gift Economy.[26] Therefore, try your best to assess all of the needs and costs associated with organizing the event, including any requests or goals for redistribution of reparations. Because we do not charge a "flat fee" in the Gift Economy, people will have questions and even some anxiety about what the "right amount" for them might be. It can be helpful to offer a few different breakdowns as a guide. (See "Resource Flow and Cost-Sharing for Events" in the Appendices for more.)

Step Three: At the event, share and discuss the vision and underlying values of gift economics. It may be helpful to distribute or display the "Principles of Gift Economics" (see the Appendices).

---

26. Winner-loser capitalism is perpetuated by a mythology which claims that certain people "deserve" more than others. Gift economics focuses on meeting genuine needs, not rewarding performance. When determining the needs you want to name, the network encourages honest conversation and introspection about the world of difference between "deserve" and "need."

The Gift Economy can only be complete when there is someone on the other side to receive the gift. We are trying to live into a worldview of abundance, where making a request and receiving people's generosity is in itself a gift that helps to complete a sacred cycle.

However, within the scarcity/capitalist system that we currently operate under, there can be a lot of shame associated with making requests for financial support, even in the form of reparations. This may be especially true for people who come from marginalized identities or a history of poverty, and could be further exacerbated if the person making the request is of a marginalized identity and the person fulfilling the request is of a privileged identity. There is an inherent power dynamic that comes into play that we should be aware of.

It is therefore important for us to create containers where people feel not only safe and protected, but invited and celebrated in making requests. This might mean creating systems for making requests privately or even anonymously.

During the presentation, openly name what the financial costs are to organize the event as well as the needs of the organizers. The needs should be written out clearly on a large piece of paper for everyone to see. Also invite people to make requests about any needs that they may have had to participate in the event that they would like to see supported (this includes reparations requests[27]). This request can be made at that moment, or later to the Money Steward one-on-one.

Step Four: At the end of the presentation, make a request for financial support from anybody who is able to give it to help meet the needs that have been shared.

Step Five: Throughout the event, continue to update the participants on how much you have collected and how close you are to meeting your goal. The updates should also be shared on the large piece of paper with the needs. Share this information as often as possible, including the final tally in any follow up communication.

---

27. Requests for reparations or financial support can be made in Step Two or Step Three of this process.

Faith in the system

Running events on a Gift Economic basis means that we have faith that in the long term our work will be sustainable. This means that some events will "pay for themselves," while other events may cost money out of our pocket, while other events will raise more than what our need was. It is important for us as the event organizers not to get discouraged if we don't bring in the total amount, and it is also important that we communicate this with the participants.

AND, as a reminder there is no one right way to do the Gift Economy. If the organizers of a particular event have needs that require reimbursement, there is nothing wrong with creating a system that asks for a minimum fee from participants.

Empire tax resistance

Members of our network are encouraged to learn about and reflect on the implications of the taxation system, and to actively discern whether they are called to refuse voluntary payment of taxes to a government devoted to war, mass incarceration, deportation, and ecological devastation. Conscientious objection to the payment of taxes and the redistribution of such funds to humane alternatives represents a longstanding nonviolence tradition. Tax resisters choose different methods. For example, some file tax forms while withholding payment, some don't file at all, and some live below the taxable income level. Some are content with resisting quietly as a personal practice, while others resist in a public way to raise awareness about the government's misuse of tax income and to outwardly demonstrate the moral power of civil disobedience.

Teams in the network are encouraged to make space for discussion and reflection about tax resistance. As with so many forms of nonviolent witness, we can accomplish so much more together than we can alone.

The National War Tax Resistance Coordinating Committee provides excellent resources for those interested in learning more about the why and how of tax resistance: `https://nwtrcc.org/`.

Information flow: how we communicate

"To create better health in a living system,
connect it to more of itself."
~ Margaret Wheatley ~

At the root of our commitment to healthy information flow is our shared understanding that decentralized groups work best when everyone takes responsibility for communicating what they notice.

Clarity about information systems (i.e., who will send and receive which kinds of information, and how) is essential to the vitality of any organization. Just as healthy nervous and circulatory systems are necessary for a human body to function well, healthy communication is necessary for an organization or team to maintain nourishing relationships, to achieve effective decision-making, and to take dynamic, inspired collective action.

It is helpful to note that feedback and conflict systems are intimately connected to the information flow system, and could in fact be viewed as subcategories of it. For that reason, descriptions of those two systems directly follow this one. Fluid, consistent, open sharing of ideas, feelings, stories, and experiences truly serves like lifeblood for our network. It would be difficult to overemphasize how closely the health of the flow of information correlates to the overall health of the network organism. In short, transparency is key, and more communication is way better than less.

Technology and information flow

We recognize that there are complexities related to technology use and information flow.

- Members of each team will have differing relationships with and differing access to tech devices and modes of communication.

- Our recommended practices attempt to accommodate different relationships with technology and access.

We respect that there are multiple ways that network members do and don't engage with different technologies. We recognize that information is power, and that limiting its accessibility can lead to holding power over or away from people in problematic ways. One example of this is the way that information flow and security measures involving the use of certain technologies invariably exclude particular people (those without smartphones and those who live rurally, for example). We encourage teams to thoughtfully consider the implications such dynamics will hold for their members and for the work they undertake together. As discussed previously we also encourage teams to carefully reflect on the impact their collective tech use has on the field they are trying to nurture.

On the matter of encryption

Because of its relevance to information flow, it's important to reiterate the gist of our thinking pertaining to security culture, with specific attention to the use of encryption. Generally speaking, our network's commitment to fierce vulnerability leads us to be as transparent as possible. Therefore, while encryption has become a commonplace security measure in many of today's movement spaces, our baseline as a network is to communicate without it. Potential exceptions might be: when the use of encryption would be tactically important to plan and pull off an action that requires enough surprise to be effective; or, when we are collaborating with other groups in the wider movement ecosystem that use encryption.

Determining your team's information flow protocol

Information flow in the network encompasses four types of communication and connection: within teams, between teams, with network collectives and with folks outside the network.

1. **Set up and maintain a consistent rhythm of team meetings.** Meetings should be frequent and regular. It is important to know the purpose of each meeting. You will often schedule meetings for planning, logistics, and decision-making; relational meetings for going deeper with practices and creating room for further connection;

and quarterly reflection circles. Every
meeting should include time for practices
that embody our network DNA. (See the
recommended practices at the end of the
Core Commitments sections.)

As a general guideline we recommend that
team meetings run for 2-3 hours in order to
leave ample time to tend to the practices
and/or business at hand, and to enjoy being
together. If weekly meetings don't work for
your team, you might alternatively choose
to meet monthly for an entire day, or twice
monthly for half-days.

2. **Decide how your team will handle day-to-day communication:**

a. What are each team member's preferred
methods of communication beyond face to
face?

b. Who is being left out of the flow of
information, and why? Access to technology? Principled abstention from
certain kinds of tech? Is your team okay
with its balance between inclusion and
exclusion?

c. What challenges have team members had
with methods of communication? How available is each person, regardless of their
methods of communication?

d. If your team has members who do not use cell phones or computers, or whose use of these is limited, what will your team do to keep them in the loop and to make sure their input is entering the system? Decide if you want someone on the team to serve as an information bridge for these teammates, and for how long they will fulfill that role.

e. What are your team's collective communication preferences? Can multiple platforms be used on your team? Who is willing to take on the responsibility to make that work?

f. Is there something other groups should know about your team's approach to communication?

g. Various members of your team will serve as links with other teams and collectives in the network, as well as with groups outside the network. These relationships are key to the team's work and will be important sources of learning for your team and for the network as a whole. Notice the way your team members' vocations fit with the groups they relate to on behalf of the team. How can your team support good information flow across this

web of connection? How can all of the
learning that's happening be harnessed
and integrated by your team and, when
applicable, by the network as a whole?

3. **Decide what your team's communication
   protocol will be for direct action scenarios**
   (as discussed in the Direct Action
   section). Establishing a baseline protocol
   for intra- and inter-team communication
   during actions is essential. This baseline
   protocol should be reviewed before each
   action, and adjusted as necessary,
   depending on the particular needs and
   circumstances of each situation. (See also
   "The field and technology use" in the
   Fierce Vulnerability section.)

4. **Set up and maintain a consistent rhythm
   of communication and connection with
   other teams.** If you are in an area with
   multiple teams, your team will collaborate
   with other teams to determine who will
   serve as links between groups to ensure
   a consistent rhythm of face-to-face team
   cluster gatherings/meetings. Perhaps
   monthly, quarterly or semi-annually. These
   meetings should include a mixture of cross-
   team relationship-building and the sharing
   of information and learning related to our
   network's core areas of experimentation.
   If your team is at a distance from

other teams, you may choose to set up a
consistent rhythm of phone or video calls
with members of other teams in the network,
geared toward the same intentions.

5. **Establish clear agreements with other
   groups you collaborate with.** While
   full transparency is our teams' baseline
   practice internally, when working with
   other groups in the movement ecosystem it
   is vital to have clear, respectful, and
   open-minded communication about our values
   and wishes with regard to communication.
   When working with others we endeavor to be
   proactive about making clear agreements.

6. **Host an open house gathering, or regular
   open house gatherings.** Hosting open
   houses is an excellent way to share about
   the network with others in the wider
   community, if/when your team has the
   capacity to do so. If you are in an area
   with multiple teams, it may be efficient to
   hold these open houses after team cluster
   meetings, so a good number of network
   members are present and so open houses are
   more easily calendared.

7. **Document key learning and information
   and share it with the network ecosystem.**
   As Margaret Wheatley says, "A living

system is a learning system." Learning from our teams' experiments with our DNA is crucial to our building a healthy and robust network that offers meaningful contributions to the struggle for justice and wholeness. For this to happen we ask our teams to prioritize the documentation of key learnings, unresolved questions, and important insights related to our network's core areas of experimentation (fierce vulnerability, direct action, reparations, vocation, emergence, and our five operational systems), and for our teams to organize that information and share it with the larger ecosystem on a regular basis. Various information flow and feedback systems are being experimented with during the soft launch, and you can also rely on the relationships you have with others in the network.

Giving and receiving feedback: how we learn from each other

"All life thrives on feedback and dies
without it."
~ Margaret Wheatley ~

A tree makes the root grow faster after detecting water. The population of bunnies increases in response to an increase in food availability, and a human gets a tummy-ache after eating a dozen snickerdoodles. That is all feedback in practice. Feedback is the way that all living systems learn and find balance.

In human social systems, feedback is equally important, and also extremely varied in its forms. It can come in the form of a certain gesture, an edit, a conversation or just a smile. Because we are alive, feedback is always happening. It can be implicit or explicit, conscious or subconscious. However, conscious and explicit feedback is important for building trust in relationships and enhancing collaboration.

Evolutionarily, our survival has largely depended on the approval of others—of being liked. For this reason, many people have developed an aversion to giving and receiving the type of feedback commonly referred to as criticism because it is often interpreted as the opposite of approval. **If we do not have a sense of**

safety and respect in a group or in a relationship, giving and receiving feedback can easily feel threatening, whether it is considered critical or complimentary. Regardless of why it has become this way, in many communities we tend to suppress this important component of life. Of course, when this happens, our learning is also suppressed.

Decentralized organizations, more than other forms of human organizations, depend heavily on the regular and clear flow of feedback. Without it, key systems of the organization will fall into ill health. Consider: What happens when I am not sure if my work is valued? Or if my voice cannot be heard? Or if I do not have a way to learn from what has happened?

Without healthy feedback, it is likely that we will lose trust, effectiveness, and coordination, and the organization will lose its ability to sense and respond. Paraphrasing Miki Kashtan of Nonviolent Global Liberation, *Whatever is not caught by the feedback system will likely manifest as conflict.*

Types of feedback

The growing root communicates to the rest of the tree that there is water, and the tree responds to that information by making the root grow even more. That is considered "positive" or **"affirming" feedback.** If the root had hit a wall instead of water, it would have set off a "negative" or **"redirecting" feedback** loop, resulting in the tree changing the course of the root's growth. In this sense, "positive" and "negative" are not value judgments. **Both types of information are valuable.**

> In our human social systems, we need both "affirming" and "redirecting" feedback, information that reinforces and amplifies our actions, and information that helps transform or redirect our actions.

Escalating conflict is an indication that the feedback process has not been sufficient or has broken down somewhere along the way. There is nothing wrong with conflict, but it does take energy and time to process. Feedback allows us to learn and adapt without having to dedicate as many resources to dealing with conflict.

Feedback process

1. **Request space and state intention:** Before offering specific feedback, ask the other person if they are available to receive it. Feedback is only helpful when both parties are prepared.

2. **Specific observations:** Identify specific behaviors at specific times that you noticed yourself. Avoid generalizations or evaluations. For example, "You left dishes in the sink" rather than "You don't care about the chore list" or "Everyone thinks you're lazy." If you tell someone that they are "mean," instead of identifying a specific behavior and sharing its

impact, they may feel the need to defend themselves. Or if you say "Your project was good" that does not help someone know what actually worked well. Being as specific as possible gives someone practical information to work with.

3. **Empathic listening**: Especially if the feedback you are offering is difficult for them to hear, maintain curiosity and, if helpful, ask them to explain the intention behind their behavior. This may help you to reach greater understanding. Try to be open to the impact of the feedback that you offered. If it is difficult for them to hear, they may benefit from you showing empathy.

4. **Explore Ideas for action**: Once mutual understanding is complete, if the recipient is open to it, you can discuss possible ways to move forward. How can this behavior be amplified, or how can it be transformed?

5. **Action plan**: Agree on a way of addressing what matters most in a way that works for everyone. If "redirecting" feedback isn't working, you might consider entering the restorative conflict engagement process.

Less structure is necessary for this process when teams share a high level of trust. When there is less trust, however, it is important to have developed and practiced these skills with some precision.

Giving feedback

Turn information into a gift. The preparation and refinement of the gift, though, must be done before approaching another person with our feedback. What can we do to help our information become really useful?

Identify the motivation for sharing information. In "Feedback Without Criticism," Miki Kashtan writes: "Providing feedback is usually motivated by a desire to contribute to the learning of another person and to the functioning of the whole. Sharing a personal trigger is usually motivated by a desire to be heard, understood, or attended to. When we mix the two, we are likely to create confusion."

Expressions that we might call "emotional discharge" offer valuable information to the system. This information is often deeper, unprocessed feedback about hurt, conflict, or not being seen.

For example: One housemate is livid when another housemate eats all of the vegan butter. The emotional response is not

---

ultimately about a huge need for vegan butter. It is deeper feedback about the vegan housemate feeling like she cannot eat comfortably in her own home or that she is experiencing feelings of being forgotten, uncared for, or unseen. So when she delivers said housemate "feedback" about butter consumption in the shared kitchen at 8:30 am with a raised voice, the core message is not actually about vegan butter it's about something more closely tied to trauma, connection, and community care.

This kind of emotional discharge will happen in our relationships. The network feedback process isn't a tool for silencing this kind of genuine expression. Instead, we hope to use these tools to process emotional discharge in productive ways, so that it can be offered as genuine feedback.

Feedback offered with these intentions helps to deepen relationships. This is a valuable offering to the whole community. Here is one way that the process of giving feedback could flow:

1. Begin by **discerning if what you have to offer is feedback**, or if it is motivated in any way by criticism, judgment or anger. There is nothing wrong with those things,

but true feedback is offered purely in the spirit of a gift.

a. Be aware of your fight/flight response, annoyance, frustration, enemy images, persistent negative judgments, reactivity or physical sensations like heat, tightness or pressure. These could be signs that there may be personal triggers getting in the way of you finding the gift.

b. If you do find that you have some charge around the incident, try to release it through empathy practices. Seek out a team member who you trust, visit a tree or another natural spot, meditate, journal, find space where you can express how you feel without blame or judgment. These practices support your process of discernment and inner clarity, as well as reconnection with the other person.

Feedback vs. Trigger

	Personal Trigger	Feedback
Needs & Intentions	Cathartic release, connection, healing	Contribute to improved function
Desired Outcome	Learning for me (& maybe other person)	Learning for other person (& maybe me)

c. If you find that there is still tension
or charge, you may want to consider
utilizing the conflict engagement
process instead.

2. Clarify your intention and message.
What is the purpose of your sharing this
feedback? Is it for the deepening of
your relationship with this person? Or to
support their growth? To support growth in
your team? It is also important to identify
specific behaviors from specific times
which relate directly to the feedback you
are giving.

3. Request space to talk and **share your
intention** (to deepen relationship, to
strengthen the team's capacity to follow
through on something, etc.).

4. Once you've received their consent, **offer
them your feedback**. Again, name specific
behaviors or actions. Share about the
impact of those behaviors or actions, and
try to be empathetic to their needs.

5. Explore ideas for action if both parties
agree that something must be done. Again,
try to be as specific as possible.

Receiving feedback

Because many of us live in a culture where there is often little discernment about the difference between true feedback and criticism, we have also subconsciously learned to resist feedback. We often see it as an attack, and we put up walls and get defensive. In doing so, we may be missing an opportunity for growth.

In addition to practicing how to give feedback, it is therefore important to practice receiving it. Here are some thoughts and practices:

1. When someone asks if you are open to receiving feedback, truly check in with yourself and make sure you have enough spaciousness to receive it.

2. Listen to the feedback and engage with it. Ask follow up questions. Make sure you understand what is being offered.

3. Work on your defensiveness and practice taking feedback in. One way to do this is by setting up role plays and inviting your teammates to give you a low-intensity form of redirecting feedback.

4. Begin to make this a regular practice in your daily life by seeking feedback from others and inviting them to offer it to you regularly.

5. Take action by receiving the feedback and thinking explicitly about how to integrate it. What changes are you going to make in your life thanks to this gift?

Learning to receive feedback without being defensive is an ongoing practice. In addition to the points above, here are three long-term things we can all practice:

1. Self acceptance: In order to be able to receive and incorporate feedback in a conscious way, we need a baseline of self-acceptance. If we are not secure in ourselves, we are much more likely to see "redirective" feedback as threatening or shame-inducing. Or, we might become overly fixated or dependent on "affirming" feedback.

2. Gratitude: Sharing feedback requires courage, honesty, and vulnerability. The person sharing feedback with you has enough respect for you to believe that sharing this information is worth it. Tap into your feelings of gratitude for this.

3. Pay attention to impact first: Sometimes feedback is intended to help us see how our behaviors have negatively impacted others. Acknowledging the impact of our actions, intentional or unintentional,

without justification, can help to give
those affected by our actions the feeling
of being heard and understood. This is
important for building trust. After
trust is developed, it might be helpful
to clarify your intent or share your
experience, if different from theirs. Only
try to do so after checking in with the
other person to see if they are willing to
hear it.

Differing feedback cultures

The way we share feedback with each other is cultural. Our personal
histories matter. For example, some children grow up in quiet
households. Some are used to frequent loud exchanges. Some people
may feel extremely uncomfortable sharing their perspective directly
and are instead accustomed to using strategies of indirect communication. Some people may be perfectly comfortable sharing their
perspectives directly, emotionally, and/or unabashedly. There are
many ways to share information, and within small subcultures many
different styles can work. In multicultural teams, however, this can
lead to misunderstandings. It is therefore helpful to explicitly name
the differences and develop commonly shared norms in order to
allow information to be exchanged in ways that are effective, and to
help us maintain healthy relationships. Be cautious of defaulting to
the norm for people with more social privilege. For example, normal-
izing discomfort with loudness can be a form of anti-Blackness or
anti-semitism.

Giving and receiving feedback is a key element of one of our core network practices. Because robust information flow and interpersonal communication are so essential to the health and vitality of the network, giving and receiving feedback is an integral part of our quarterly team reflection circles.

Restorative conflict engagement: how we fight and make up

"Conflict is the spirit of the relationship asking itself to deepen."

~ Sobonfu Somé ~

Conflict is a natural and inevitable part of human interactions. It is neither good nor bad, only something that arises when the needs of two or more people are unmet or seem to be incompatible. Though it always includes some level of discomfort, we can deal with that discomfort in ways that are constructive, harmful, or a mix of the two. Many of us have learned to associate conflict with "dominant culture" strategies: shaming, avoiding, pay-back, arguing, fighting and blaming. However, those things are not actually conflicts—rather they are limited strategies that we can use to respond to conflicts. It is just as possible, however, for the same conflict to lead to a deepening of connection and understanding. If we do not have explicit agreements about how to address conflict in healthy ways, when we are under stress we are likely to default to the common and harmful ways of handling it.

When two people are in conflict, it is helpful to remember that it is the two of them versus the problem, not one person versus the other.

Trauma and conflict

We dealt with the topic of trauma in some depth in the Fierce Vulnerability section. It is deeply important, though, to revisit the fact that the trauma we carry in our bodies and psyches resurfaces when triggered by new events. This is especially true in the case of conflicts. When conflict triggers past trauma we are faced with the double challenge of not only finding reconciliation in the current conflict but also moving through physical sensations and subconscious and compounded emotions that are associated with past experiences. We all carry unique personal and historical/intergenerational traumas in our bodies, and these unfortunately make us prone to a shame/blame mindset.

With that as a backdrop, it comes as no surprise that dealing with past trauma is all but inevitable in group settings, and that the surfacing of trauma is typically compounded the more varied groups are in terms of identity expression.

Healing from trauma is deep, long-term work. For substantial trauma to be processed well, instead of causing more trauma for the individual and community, robust systems of support and training are essential. Teams are strongly encouraged to self-assess their aptitude in terms of holding and working with trauma, to do the level of work they're capable of on their own, and to seek out the guidance and resources they need beyond that.

Teams are also encouraged to develop the courageous capacity to lovingly name when the present trauma is more than they're able to adequately tend. In such cases it is vital to ask for help.

Breaking free from the cycle of trauma and shame

All of us have been traumatized living within a dehumanizing and genocidal civilization. This trauma is too often perpetuated and passed on through the weapon of shame. Having seen the toxic and paralyzing effect of a culture of shaming on activist communities, as we engage with one another to transform the conflicts that arise between us, we commit to doing everything we can to not perpetuate trauma and shame. We strive to honor each other's trauma with empathy, and rather than internalizing and passing on that trauma, we seek to hold it with compassion and love. We commit to not forgetting the injustices that have caused trauma, while remembering how easily we ourselves can justify harming others. Resisting the tendency toward shame allows us the space for the difficult process of being accountable for genuine guilt, repentance, and healing.

Restorative conflict engagement processes

To free up our creativity and courage when conflict arises, each team must develop shared commitments about how to deal with conflict. This document offers an initial set of processes to support restorative approaches to conflict engagement. We invite people to apply these practices **with the conscious intention to transform interpersonal tension into an opportunity for healing and learning**, instead of blaming and separation. Engaging in conflict, rather than avoiding it, creates space for important feedback to make its way into the relationship/team.

In discussing conflict, it's important to note that different individuals, communities and cultures can define and respond to conflict very differently. What is considered "conflict" in one community might be experienced as a "lively discussion" in another. Likewise, some cultures typically engage tension very openly and directly, while in other groups there may be a strong encouragement to focus on social cohesion and minimize dissent. This diversity invites us to approach disagreement with humility and an awareness of multiple perspectives.

A written description of conflict engagement processes should be accessible for everyone to read at all times, including identification of a few skilled facilitators, how to initiate your chosen practices, how to support your facilitators, and, if possible, a neutral, dedicated place for meetings to transform conflict. If applicable, a dedicated online platform can also be identified for times when an in-person process is not possible or appropriate.

When you notice conflict between yourself and others, practice fierce vulnerability. The following are the baseline elements of our network's conflict engagement system. We invite you to replace these with other practices that meet the same goals, and which may be more culturally relevant to your team.

1. **Develop awareness and self-empathy:** Everything starts with active awareness that you are feeling tension. Notice it, see if you can place it in your body. What does this tension feel like? See if you can have awareness about the roots of this tension. How much of it is a direct result of your interaction with this other person, and how much of it is something deeper inside you that was triggered by that interaction? Give yourself empathy and compassion for whatever feelings you may be having. Give yourself space to feel them.

2. **Releasing the charge and empathic listening:** Try to release as much of the charge as possible before engaging. Writing about it, talking to a trusted friend or teammate, going for a walk, meditating or hitting a punching bag can all be helpful tools to release some of the charge. Practices in the Giving and Receiving Feedback section may also be helpful.

3. **Preparations for dialog:** In general, if we want to engage in an extended dialog with someone to resolve a conflict, it is really

helpful to have already been practicing feedback sharing in other contexts, preferably in an ongoing way.

4. **Direct dialog**: The dialog process is a chance for both parties to be heard and understood, to support healing. This conversation is supported by mutual curiosity to understand and learn from each other, and it is worth celebrating simply arriving at it. Take turns speaking while using statements that begin with I, without interrupting, continuing until both sides have a sense of being understood. You can reflect back what you heard ("I heard you say…") or ask reflective questions (Are you saying…?) to test for shared understanding. Then see if either of you have specific offers or requests for restorative action and/or future agreements to help one another stay the course. It can also be supportive to plan to check back with each other 24 hours later to see if anything else has arisen. If after 10-15 minutes the dialog is not going well for either (or both) of you, look for support and either return to step 1 or move to step 5.

5. **Supported dialog**:

   a. **Facilitation**: Bring in a third party that you both agree on to help with the conflict. A third party facilitator can support conscious dialog between the two parties, contributing their presence as needed to support reconciliation, from silent witnessing to active mediation. This conversation can be organic or you can agree on a process like reflective listening or another format. The responsibility of the third party should be clear to everyone involved. Are they just providing an empathic container and silently listening? Or are they also helping translate what the two parties are actually saying, and/or providing their feedback/opinion/advice?

b. Community circle process: In many cases, a community co-creates conflict and is affected by it, and thus can also co-create new conditions to better meet everyone's needs. When a conflict has more intensity or relevance for multiple people in a community, someone may initiate some form of community-run process for restoring connection and trust. As each team designs systems for conflict restoration, it may want to consider questions such as: How will the process work? (e.g. whether all network community members are informed of each circle; whether everyone can opt in or out; what to do if someone opts out;

what you want facilitators to do and not
do, etc.); How will the two parties in
conflict support those who facilitate the
community circle?; Where will your circle
be held?; How are circles initiated?
How will the team/community make sure
that everyone involved understands this
process and has access to it? Processes
may include restorative models like
"talking stick" or "fishbowl" process.
If this process does not bring about the
resolution desired, go to step 6.

6. **Outside support**: Call in an outside
conflict engagement team that the key
people involved trust and which has been
decided in advance. This may be people
within or outside the larger network
ecosystem or others that have been referred
to you. Make sure this team understands
exactly how you want them to support you
in engaging with the conflict. Get clear on
the process and the role you want them to
play before inviting them in.

In the case of a serious breach of network DNA

In most cases, if someone believes that it is important for another person to leave the team due to a serious breach of core network agreements, they will seek advice from fellow teammates, as well as enter into the restorative conflict engagement process. Hopefully this process will restore enough trust to repair the breach, and the member's removal will not need to be considered.

If the conflict engagement process does not bring about the needed level of repair, and a more in-depth restorative pathway is called for, we ask that the following guidelines be followed:

1. The team member in question will take a break from active participation on the team, and will choose two willing sponsors/ support people from the team or from the team's network community to accompany them through the following steps.

2. The team member will find people who are skilled in the area where the breach has occurred and will work with everyone to bring healing when ready.

3. If and when restoration has happened to a point that all parties are satisfied, the person may become an active part in the team's network community (maintaining active relationship with their sponsors).

4. After a minimum of a six-month period of active participation in the network community, they can start the onboarding process again. After completing the onboarding process, they can rejoin their team, if everyone is in agreement, or join/form a new team. This entire process will include the ongoing support and friendship of the sponsors.

5. If the breach of core agreements happens again, the restorative pathway becomes a longer and more robust process.

Dismissal from the network

It is possible that a member has to be asked to leave their team and the network indefinitely because of acts or an act that breach(es) core agreements in an extremely harmful way (i.e., sexual or physical violence, theft from a team or collective, consistent acts to undermine relationships, continued breach of agreements related to reparations and action time, or consistent unwillingness to receive and integrate feedback). In such cases the team(s) and network members involved are asked to be in conversation with other network members outside of your team for guidance and an outside perspective, including members who may have experience or expertise in the specific kinds of harm that may have occurred. Together, a process for the members' dismissal and a process for healing for those who have been harmed will be co-created.

The essential role of trust and connection

While conflict is a natural part of community, cultivating trust and connection can help reduce its intensity and the harmful or unhelpfully disruptive impacts of conflict unskillfully managed. Cultivating trust and connection can also help in deepening relationships among team members on two sides of a conflict when the conflict has been formally resolved by the team (with respect to reaching a decision that enables the team to proceed with their work) but the relationships have not been adequately restored.

Here are some suggestions for ways to cultivate trust and connection on your team:

1. Sing songs, make music or other arts and crafts together;

2. Play or share physical work together;

3. Exchange empathic listening;

4. Share spiritual practices such as meditation, prayer, yoga, etc.;

5. Hear each other's life stories;

6. Share food together;

7. Share safe touch;

8. Share laughter;

9. Time in silence or nature together;

10. Rest

Conflict engagement is a key element of one of our core network practices. The conflict engagement processes detailed above provide a baseline structure for all network members to employ when conflict arises, except in cases where teams have developed their own alternative model. Because conflict engagement is so essential to the health and vitality of the network, it is an integral part of our quarterly team reflection circles.

APPENDICES

Core Network Practices
Reparations self-audit

We recommend creating a field together when your team discusses their individual experiences completing the self-audit. Elements of ceremony can help heal and deepen relationships ruptured by racial and class oppression. Candles, food, and a grounding are all suggested for this practice.

Part 1: Ancestry and history

1. Where do your ancestors come from? How did you come to be born or raised where you were or to live on the land you are on today?

2. *Enslavement*:
   a. If you have family with histories of enslaving people, what more can you learn about that history?
   b. If you have family with histories of being enslaved, what more can you learn about that history?

3. *White settler colonization of Indigenous lands*:
   a. If you have white settler ancestors, what have you learned about their histories of settlement on Indigenous lands? Can you name the ways your family benefited from this settlement? How might you learn more?
   b. If you have Indigenous ancestors, what have you learned about their histories? How might you learn more?
   c. Is there any other relevant history of colonization in your family that falls outside these two categories? What do you know about this history in your family, and how can you learn more?

4. *Immigration*: If applicable, what is the immigration story of your family? What class or socio-economic background did they come from in the places from which they emigrated?

5. *Resistance*: Have you investigated and reclaimed histories of resistance within and across your family and ancestral lines? Who are the people and what are the stories of resistance that empower you from within your family and ancestry?

Part 2: Access to financial security

1. What is your income? Is this from a salary, hourly work or another source? Do you anticipate maintaining/increasing/decreasing this earning in the time ahead?

    a. If sharing income with a partner, what is your shared income? (Apply questions below to your shared financial situation, as is relevant.)

    b. What industry does your income come from? How is money generated in this industry? What impacts does it have on workers/land/society, now and in the past?

    c. What is your percentile (e.g. "Are you in the 1%?") for your age by income? Use this tool: https://bit.ly/3w7zsjm.

2. What are your expenses? Do you plan for them to increase or decrease in the time ahead?

3. How many people are financially dependent on you (children, siblings, parents, extended or chosen family)?

4. How old are you? Do you anticipate "retiring"?

5. Do you have savings? How many months of your expenses do your savings represent?

6. Do you have invested assets, including retirement funds, or do you own land/property?

    a. How are these assets invested? What impact do these investments have on workers/land/society?

7. Do you have debt? What is this debt from?

8. Net wealth is a representation of more than your current income. It is calculated by adding your savings and assets and then subtracting your debt (savings + assets - debt). What percentile are you by net wealth? Use this tool: https://bit.ly/3jvOQ6o

9. How have you paid for any higher education, private schooling, or specialized training?

10. Do you have more or less money than your parents do/did while you were a child?

11. Have you ever inherited money? Do you expect to in the future? Where did this money come from?

12. Do you or does anyone in your family currently redistribute money? To where or who? How much? Why?

13. If married or sharing resources with anyone: Do they have access to more or less financial resources than you?

Part 3: Lived experience

1. How many days a month do you spend worrying about money? How does this impact you?

2. Do you believe you have ever been turned down for an opportunity, or paid less, based on your identity?

3. Regardless of what's in your wallet or bank account, do you experience that you have a financial safety net because of your family or other social connections?

4. Are the choices you are making with money helping to build the kind of world you want to live in?

5. How comfortable/uncomfortable is doing this audit for you? Do you have a sense of why that is?

Part 4: Making reparations real[28] (personal)

Personal reparations practice, likely as a BIPOC member of the network:

1. If you are interested in receiving reparations, how will you communicate that with your teammates and/or the rest of the community? How can relationships be strengthened by making reparations real within your team or community? What other conversations or support would you like to have with your team and/or the rest of the community to make it possible?

---

28. See "Positionality" in the Reparations section for related discussion.

2. If you are more focused on directing the flow of reparations than receiving those resources yourself, how will you share your ideas and commitments with your team and/or the broader network?

3. If you feel called to redistribute your resources, why? How much of your income/wealth are you considering redistributing, and to whom? Some of the questions that follow for white-identified members may also be supportive for you to consider.

Personal reparations practice, likely as a white member of the network:

1. Redistribute enough that it feels risky—if you feel comfortable, you're likely not stretching enough. If you feel destabilized, it might be too much.
   a. One way to do this: Choose a random number and see what feelings arise for you (is it scary? exciting? uninspiring?)— and then increase or decrease that number and see how your feelings change.
   b. See if you can identify a number that feels like an edge for positive challenge and growth.

2. Choose a politically significant percentage of your income or wealth. Perhaps using statistics around earning potential across race in your chosen field, in your region, or in the US, etc.

3. Double what you gave away last year, and redistribute that amount as a reparations commitment.

4. Choose an amount that will make you feel invested in the person, movement or organization to which you offer reparations.

5. Get inspiration from your religious tradition (e.g., the Christian practice of tithing, the Jewish commitment to Tzedakah, and the Muslim call to Zaka).

6. Check out the average amount that people in your income bracket redistribute, and try doubling it. This article can help: https://bit.ly/3dqnz11.

7. Choose an amount that will make you feel like you've really showed up.

8. For those with high-net wealth, choose a time frame within which you will redistribute all excess wealth you hold.
   a. If you have invested assets, begin by saying no to making wealth off of wealth
      i. Redistribute all capital gains by offering a minimum of 7% of your total assets as reparations annually.
      ii. Consider alternative investments that build community rather than corporate wealth. Find good possibilities here: https://bit.ly/31rQT59.
   b. For those acquiring wealth through highly paid work, redistribute all wealth above a moderate standard of living.
   c. Don't forget about land, property or other physical assets. What do you "own" that could transfer in ownership to Black or Indigenous people? Until that time, how can these assets be of deeper service to movements while under your stewardship?

Part 5: Making reparations real (systemic)

1. How familiar are you with the history of the reparations struggle in the US and the groups that have carried that struggle forward? Have particular resources been especially meaningful to you in your learning process about this history? If not, are you ready and willing to dive into some of the resources listed at the end of this handbook?

2. How familiar are you with contemporary systemic reparations victories? Are you aware, for example, of recent reparations breakthroughs in Asheville, NC, Evanston, IL, or Oakland, CA? Do you know about Chicago's pivotal and comprehensive 2015 reparations legislation benefitting victims of police torture?
   a. If so, what do you find particularly inspiring about these efforts?
   b. If not, are you ready to investigate these historic initiatives?

3. What do you know about current reparations organizations, legislation, campaigns, etc., in or beyond your locale?

    a. Do you feel drawn to involvement (or deeper involvement) with one or more of these efforts?

        i. If so, do you want to propose that your team considers getting involved with you?

4. Do you yourself have a vision or the beginning of a vision for a project or campaign seeking systemic reparations gains?

    a. If so, are you ready to plant the seed of this vision with your teammates?

The network gratefully acknowledges the following resources for helping us create this audit:

- Resource Generation—https://resourcegeneration.org/
- Give Big Now, Keep Giving for Social Justice—https://bit.ly/3w-8ZoLm
- Giving Guidelines—https://bit.ly/3qE2lCw
- Coming to the Table—https://comingtothetable.org/
- Reparations: The Time Is Now!—https://bit.ly/2TbcURD
- How to Give Away Money by Holly Fetter—https://bit.ly/3Jp-cMSo

Direct action resources

There are a great many resources on direct action and campaigning, several of which we've cited throughout the handbook. See also the Additional Resources section later in these Appendices, and the Direct Action Manual created by the Climate Disobedience Center, available here: `https://bit.ly/3qKd7aM`. This manual elaborates on the resources covered here, and provides much more information on a variety of related topics—from campaign timelines to how to debrief an action to offering jail support.

This section will offer just a few resources that we think are essential as you begin to plan out your direct actions.

Points of intervention

Local governments, state violence, and the corporate capture of policy have consistently created and upheld systemic violence toward brown and Black communities. Our racial healing and climate justice commitments are best served when we choose points of intervention accordingly. Teams are encouraged to ask themselves: What points of intervention will support our most impacted communities to build the power and capacity needed to overcome oppression.

Points of Intervention examples: fossil fuel industry[29]

Consider the following potential settings for direct action:

- Our dependence on oil starts with the belief that we need oil to provide energy, that we need oil to fuel our cars—or deeper still, that we need to drive cars—and that alternative energy sources are not effective or don't exist. We call this the **Point of Assumption**. It is the point where social norms are developed and upheld.

- The **Point of Destruction** is where resources are extracted and pollution is released. In this case, this is where the oil is drilled.

---

29. Read more on the Beautiful Trouble website: `https://beautiful trouble.org/theory/points-of-intervention/`

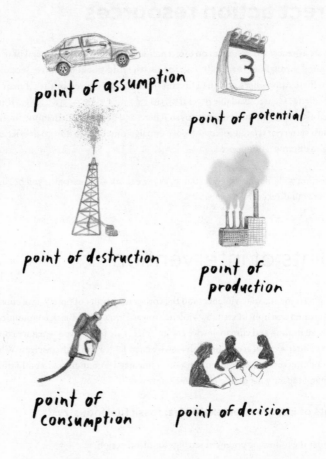

point of assumption

point of potential

point of destruction

point of production

point of consumption

point of decision

- Then the oil is piped to refineries, where it is prepared for use in products and for sale on the market. This is the **Point of Production**—where harmful items are created.

- Next, the oil is sold in the form of plastics, engine oil, gasoline, etc. This is the **Point of Consumption**, where products reach the consumer.

- Then there's the **Point of Disposal**. For example, many communities across broad swathes of the US are forced into becoming points of disposal for the pipeline industry. A massive amount of environmental and social degradation occurs due to waste generated not just by the pipelines themselves but through the disposal of the materials used in the extraction process.

- At big gatherings like oil company shareholder meetings or "free trade" summits, government and corporate representatives make decisions to expand oil extraction, or reduce trade barriers to make it easier for oil companies to establish a presence in other markets. This is the **Point of Decision**—where plans for the future are determined.

- Lastly, consider the **Point of Potential**—times when, for cultural or historical reasons, particular moments become action opportunities. With oil, some Points of Potential include Earth Day, the anniversary of the War in Iraq, or Veterans Day.

Spectrum of allies

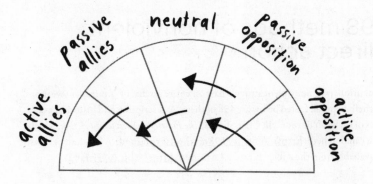

In most social change campaigns it's not necessary to win active opponents over to your point of view, even if the opponent is the target. It's only necessary to move each of the pie wedges—see illustration above—one step in your direction. If you can convince your passive allies to become active, the neutrals to become your passive allies, and the passive opponents to act neutrally—you can achieve your aims.

Here is an example from a Student Nonviolent Coordinating Committee (SCLC) organizer, Bernard Lafayette, describing SCLC's efforts to register voters in Selma, Alabama, in 1965:

> We tried to get people around the city to come, but it was slow. So we went out in the rural [areas]. The people out there are close to the earth, they're very religious and warm and friendly. And mostly they're unafraid. They own most

of their own property and their little stores. So we got these people to go and try to register to vote.

Then we used this as leverage to try to embarrass many of the people in the city. City folks are sometimes critical and skeptical about country people. So we pointed out that these people were really getting ahead. When these city people began to go down it was really sort of a birth of a movement.[30]

In this case, going after a group that was easier to reach (rural folks) made it more possible to mobilize a more difficult group (city folks). At other times, one might choose to reach out to harder-to-mobilize groups first.

For more on spectrum of allies, including detailed instructions for how to use it, see: https://beautifulrising.org/tool/spectrum-of-allies

198 methods of nonviolent direct action

Practitioners of nonviolent struggle have an entire arsenal of "nonviolent weapons" at their disposal. Listed below are 198 of them. A description and historical examples of each can be found in Gene Sharp's, *The Politics of Nonviolent Action*, which you can find here: https://cutt.ly/198methodsexplained. A handout of this list is available from the Albert Einstein Institute at https://bit.ly/3jrfsFT.

---

30. Excerpt from a resource by Joshua Kahn Russell and Daniel Hunter (www.trainingforchange.org). SNCC story from Guy and Candie Carawan, ed., *Sing for Freedom: The Story of the Civil Rights Movement Through its Songs*, NewSouth Books, 2007.

THE METHODS OF NONVIOLENT PROTEST AND PERSUASION

Formal Statements
1. Public Speeches
2. Letters of opposition or support
3. Declarations by organizations and institutions
4. Signed public statements
5. Declarations of indictment and intention
6. Group or mass petitions

Communications with a Wider Audience
7. Slogans, caricatures, and symbols
8. Banners, posters, and displayed communications
9. Leaflets, pamphlets, and books
10. Newspapers and journals
11. Records, radio, and television
12. Skywriting and earthwriting

Group Representations
13. Deputations
14. Mock awards
15. Group lobbying
16. Picketing
17. Mock elections

Symbolic Public Acts
18. Displays of flags and symbolic colors
19. Wearing of symbols
20. Prayer and worship
21. Delivering symbolic objects
22. Protest disrobing
23. Destruction of own property
24. Symbolic lights

25. Displays of portraits
26. Paint as protest
27. New signs and names
28. Symbolic sounds
29. Symbolic reclamations
30. Rude gestures

Pressures on Individuals
31. "Haunting" officials
32. Taunting officials
33. Fraternization
34. Vigils

Drama and Music
35. Humorous skits and pranks
36. Performances of plays and music
37. Singing

Processions
38. Marches
39. Parades
40. Religious processions
41. Pilgrimages
42. Motorcades

Honoring the Dead
43. Political mourning
44. Mock funerals
45. Demonstrative funerals
46. Homage at burial places

Public Assemblies
47. Assemblies of protest or support
48. Protest meetings
49. Camouflaged meetings of protest
50. Teach-ins

Withdrawal and Renunciation

51. Walk-outs
52. Silence
53. Renouncing honors
54. Turning one's back

THE METHODS OF SOCIAL NONCOOPERATION

Ostracism of Persons

55. Social boycott
56. Selective social boycott
57. Lysistratic nonaction
58. Excommunication
59. Interdict

Noncooperation with Social Events, Customs, and Institutions

60. Suspension of social and sports activities
61. Boycott of social affairs
62. Student strike
63. Social disobedience
64. Withdrawal from social institutions

Withdrawal from the Social System

65. Stay-at-home
66. Total personal noncooperation
67. "Flight" of workers
68. Sanctuary
69. Collective disappearance
70. Protest emigration (hijrat)

THE METHODS OF ECONOMIC NON-COOPERATION: ECONOMIC BOYCOTTS

Actions by Consumers

71. Consumers' boycott
72. Nonconsumption of boycotted goods
73. Policy of austerity
74. Rent withholding
75. Refusal to rent
76. National consumers' boycott
77. International consumers' boycott

Action by Workers and Producers

78. Workmen's boycott
79. Producers' boycott

Action by Middlemen

80. Suppliers' and handlers' boycott

Action by Owners and Management

81. Traders' boycott
82. Refusal to let or sell property
83. Lockout
84. Refusal of industrial assistance
85. Merchants' "general strike"

Action by Holders of Financial Resources

86. Withdrawal of bank deposits
87. Refusal to pay fees, dues, and assessment
88. Refusal to pay debts or interest
89. Severance of funds and credit
90. Revenue refusal
91. Refusal of a government's money

Action by Governments

92. Domestic embargo
93. Blacklisting of traders
94. International sellers' embargo
95. International buyers' embargo
96. International trade embargo

THE METHODS OF ECONOMIC NON-COOPERATION: THE STRIKE

Symbolic Strikes

97. Protest strike
98. Quickie walkout (lightning strike agricultural strikes)
99. Peasant strike
100. Farm workers' strike / strikes by special groups
101. Refusal of impressed labor
102. Prisoners' strike
103. Craft strike
104. Professional strike

Ordinary Industrial Strikes

105. Establishment strike
106. Industry strike
107. Sympathetic strike

Restricted Strikes

108. Detailed strike
109. Bumper strike
110. Slowdown strike
111. Working-to-rule strike
112. Reporting "sick" (sick-in)
113. Strike by resignation
114. Limited strike
115. Selective strike

Multi-Industry Strikes

116. Generalized strike
117. General strike

Combination of Strikes and Economic Closures

118. Hartal
119. Economic shutdown

THE METHODS OF POLITICAL NON-COOPERATION

Rejection of Authority

120. Withholding or withdrawal of allegiance
121. Refusal of public support
122. Literature and speeches advocating resistance

Citizens' Noncooperation with Government

123. Boycott of legislative bodies
124. Boycott of elections
125. Boycott of government employment and positions
126. Boycott of government depts., agencies, and other bodies
127. Withdrawal from government educational institutions
128. Boycott of government-supported organizations

129. Refusal of assistance to enforcement agents
130. Removal of own signs and placemarks
131. Refusal to accept appointed officials
132. Refusal to dissolve existing institutions

Citizens' Alternatives to Obedience

133. Reluctant and slow compliance
134. Nonobedience in absence of direct supervision
135. Popular nonobedience
136. Disguised disobedience
137. Refusal of an assemblage or meeting to disperse
138. Sitdown
139. Noncooperation with conscription and deportation
140. Hiding, escape, and false identities
141. Civil disobedience of "illegitimate" laws

Action by Government Personnel

142. Selective refusal of assistance by government aides
143. Blocking of lines of command and information
144. Stalling and obstruction
145. General administrative noncooperation
146. Judicial noncooperation
147. Deliberate inefficiency and selective noncooperation by enforcement agents
148. Mutiny

Domestic Governmental Action

149. Quasi-legal evasions and delays
150. Noncooperation by constituent governmental units

International Governmental Action

151. Changes in diplomatic and other representations
152. Delay and cancellation of diplomatic events
153. Withholding of diplomatic recognition
154. Severance of diplomatic relations
155. Withdrawal from international organizations
156. Refusal of membership in international bodies
157. Expulsion from international organizations

THE METHODS OF NON-VIOLENT INTERVENTION

Psychological Intervention

158. Self-exposure to the elements
159. The fast
    a) Fast of moral pressure
    b) Hunger strike
    c) Satyagrahic fast
160. Reverse trial
161. Nonviolent harassment

Physical Intervention

162. Sit-in
163. Stand-in
164. Ride-in
165. Wade-in
166. Mill-in
167. Pray-in
168. Nonviolent raids
169. Nonviolent air raids
170. Nonviolent invasion

171. Nonviolent interjection
172. Nonviolent obstruction
173. Nonviolent occupation

Social Intervention
174. Establishing new social patterns
175. Overloading of facilities
176. Stall-in
177. Speak-in
178. Guerrilla theater
179. Alternative social
180. Alternative communication system

Economic Intervention
181. Reverse strike
182. Stay-in strike
183. Nonviolent land seizure
184. Defiance of blockades
185. Politically motivated counterfeiting
186. Preclusive purchasing
187. Seizure of assets
188. Dumping
189. Selective patronage
190. Alternative markets
191. Alternative transportation systems
192. Alternative economic institutions

Political Intervention
193. Overloading of administrative systems
194. Disclosing identities of secret agents
195. Seeking imprisonment
196. Civil disobedience of "neutral" laws
197. Work-on without collaboration
198. Dual sovereignty and parallel
    government

Nonviolence International has developed an
updated list with over 300 tactics, at:

https://bit.ly/3waLFqM

Action agreements

Action agreements are an important part of preparing for an action. They can remind participants why they are there, create a sense of unity and discipline, and help to ensure our shared commitment to integral nonviolence and fierce vulnerability.

Below are sample action agreements used by the No Coal No Gas (NCNG) Campaign. This version is edited for brevity. The full version—including adaptations for actions during the COVID-19 pandemic—can be viewed at https://cutt.ly/NoCoalNoGasAgreements

These agreements are a distillation of our community's values. By participating in this action, you consent to follow these agreements, and to be called back into these agreements with love if you step out of them. Mistakes happen, we are all human, and we agree to hold one another accountable to these commitments with love and respect. For each action, participants may be asked to affirm additional agreements relevant to safety or strategy for specific scenarios.

1. I will stay safe. This includes:
   a. I will have a buddy and we will stay together.
   b. I will come prepared for the weather.
   c. If I plan to risk arrest, I will complete an action support form.

2. I will be aware of the whole group and act as a team. This includes:
   a. I will watch for those who could be in danger, left behind, or at higher risk than they want to.
   b. I will ask for help when I need it.
   c. I will give help when others ask.
   d. I will follow decisions made by the process agreed upon by the group.
   e. I will only do as much as I'm able and called to do; I will not push myself or others beyond our limits.
   f. I will be mindful of how my actions impact the safety of others, including how I act toward law enforcement.

3. I will follow the action plan. This includes:
   a. I will not lie to the police (it's OK to remain silent).

b. I will not initiate touch with the police, their property, or their vehicles.

c. I will refer police to the police liaison/de-escalator on the team.

d. If I bring a phone, it will be locked with a method OTHER THAN fingerprint or facial recognition.

e. I will not wear a mask or in any other way attempt to hide my identity.

4. I will follow the messaging plan.

5. I will remain physically and verbally nonviolent. Examples:

a. Verbal: I will not communicate in ways that dehumanize or threaten others. This includes in-person and digital communications.

b. Physical: I will not throw things. I will not touch others without their consent. I will not physically assault or threaten to physically assault anyone.

6. I will not be under the influence of or in possession of illegal drugs, marijuana, or alcohol, and I will not carry a weapon.

a. If I plan to use an item during the action that may be construed as a weapon, I will check in with the police liaison team and tactical leads about how best to handle this object if approached by police or security.

7. I will act with respect and equity toward others, being aware of varied identities and experiences within our group and beyond.

a. I will be aware of the dynamics of gender, race, and class within our group and act to break down systems of oppression where I see them.

b. I will not use racist or culturally appropriative words or symbols in any communication.

8. I will act from my heart & my conviction and stay connected to that which called me here.

Quarterly team reflection circle

Note: After teams have become well accustomed to this circle practice, they are invited to adapt this practice to meet their needs.

Prior to attending the reflection circle, it can be supportive for everyone attending the circle to take time to make notes on their responses to the questions below, both in relation to their own self-reflection, and in offering reflection to other circle members.

As with other kinds of meetings, it serves to start with a brief check-in, to identify a facilitator (to track time and the flow of the process) and a notetaker (so the "focus person" can be present and has a record of reflections and an action plan after the circle), and to end with a check-out on how the process was for everyone. The heart of a reflection circle consists of three stages for each person, with the focus person receiving the circle's attention and reflection: 1) self-reflection; 2) circle reflection; and 3) action plan.

1. **Self-reflection:** (~5 minutes) The focus person shares self-reflection on their contributions and growth edges in relation to the purpose and values of the team and the network. It can be useful to consider areas of content, process and interpersonal interaction. Self-reflection questions:

    o   What am I appreciating about how I have shown up for or contributed to this team?

    o   Do I have any regrets about the impact of how I have shown up (or not shown up) in relation to this team?

    o   What interpersonal disconnects or tensions do I have, or have I had, with others on this team? What is the state of these relationships at this time?

    o   What do I see as my areas of learning and growth in contributing to this team?

2. **Circle reflections:** (~2-3 minutes per person) The members of the circle then do a round of responses and additions to what the focus person has shared, practicing being kind, supportive and self-responsible, without compromising what is true for them. They share their own observations and experience of the focus person's contributions and growth edges in relation to the purpose

and values of the team and the network, perhaps affirming some of what has already been shared, perhaps adding things that the focus person did not mention which they find significant. It can be useful to include both general assessments (while making clear that they are not absolute truth) and specific examples for illustration. Describe the impact of the focus person's actions and way of being. Again, it can be useful to consider areas of content, process and interpersonal interaction. The invitation is to reflect with a clear intention to contribute to connection and learning, and with attunement to the individual's willingness and capacity to receive reflections, as well as care for the integrity of the community and its purpose. Circle reflection questions:

o   What am I appreciating about how I have experienced this person showing up for or contributing to this team?

o   Are there impacts of how this person has shown up (or not shown up) in relation to this team that I would like acknowledged?

o   What interpersonal disconnects or tensions does this person have, or have they had, with others on this team? What is the state of these relationships at this time?

o   What do I see as this person's areas of learning and growth in contributing to this team?

Additionally, the "focus person" can then reflect back what they heard from the circle, to make sure it has been received and to reinforce it.

3. **Action plan:** (~5-10 minutes) Integrating all of these reflections and with the support of the circle, the individual creates and commits to an Action Plan of specific time-bound actions and practices to support their further growth and embodiment in relation to the purpose and values of the team and the network. The members of the circle make requests and suggestions of the focus person, as well as the focus person volunteering their own offers and agreements. Record the actions that have been voluntarily agreed upon, who has agreed to them, and the agreed upon time frames for all actions. Action plan questions:

    o   What would I like to see happen in relation to all that has been shared? How can any needed restoration or repair happen? What would I like to offer or request? What do I agree to do? With what timeframe?

The process then moves to the next "focus person" until everyone has had their turn. It is important to leave ample time for this process so that insight and connection have the time they need to emerge. Take breaks as needed. Depending on the circumstances, multiple meetings may be needed for everyone in the group to have their turn.

End with a check-out, sharing how the process was for everyone involved.

Team rounds (to be included at least on an annual basis)

After the Personal Rounds, the circle moves on to the Team Rounds, going around the circle for Step 4, the Team Reflection Round, and then going around the circle a final time for Step 5, the Team Action Plan.

4. Team reflection round: (~5 minutes per person)
- What am I celebrating and/or appreciating about this team?

- What am I mourning, challenged by and/or concerned about as a member of this team?

- What disconnects or tensions are present for me, or have been present for me, as a member of this team? What is the state of these tensions at this time?

- What is my vision of how I'd love to experience this team functioning?

5. Team action plan round: (~10-20 minutes)
- What would I like to see happen in relation to all that has been shared? How can any needed restoration or repair happen? What would I like to offer or request? What do I agree to do? With what timeframe?

Further recommendation

All individuals currently or formerly involved with the network, particularly who are not currently a part of a team or collective, are strongly encouraged to initiate a reflection circle with a group of individuals with whom they have worked most closely within the network, as soon as possible.

An Aspirational Vision of a National Structure

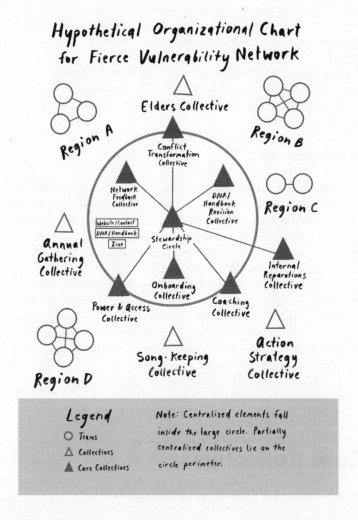

Hypothetical Organizational Chart for Fierce Vulnerability Network

Elders Collective

Region A

Region B

Conflict Transformation Collective

Network Feedback Collective

DNA/ Handbook Revision Collective

Region C

Website/Contact
DNA/Handbook
Zine

Stewardship Circle

Annual Gathering Collective

Internal Reparations Collective

Onboarding Collective

Power & access Collective

Coaching Collective

Song-Keeping Collective

Action Strategy Collective

Region D

Legend
○ Teams
△ Collectives
▲ Core Collectives

Note: Centralized elements fall inside the large circle. Partially centralized collectives lie on the circle perimeter.

During the last phase of DNA-building leading up to the publication of this handbook, network DNA builders developed the above illustration of a hypothetical national structure for FVN. The purpose of this exercise was to envision the structures that would be needed to adequately support the type of team clusters we anticipate will come into being in different regions around the country.

The DNA builders believed that the core collectives depicted in this organizational chart would be most essential to the health and vitality of a national (and potentially international) FVN. At the time of this writing, however, we have determined that the network does not have the capacity to populate and implement these core collectives. We include descriptions of them below in order to provide a more thorough aspirational picture of a national structure that our unofficial beta-testing teams can keep in mind during the network's "soft launch" phase. Perhaps this aspirational picture represents a direction we want to head in as we build, grow and experiment together.

Though these core collectives were originally envisioned as national structures, we encourage teams to experiment with similar structures at the local level. Our local learning will inform what we may choose to try nationally (and perhaps, eventually, internationally).

Two Clarifications:

In the following descriptions, "centralized" signifies the expectation that all teams in the network would interact with the collective across the breadth of its functions. "Partially centralized" means that all teams in the network would interact with some functions of the collective, but not necessarily all of them. And "not centralized" means that teams would be at liberty to choose for themselves whether or not they interact with the collective, and to what extent.

Also, please bear in mind that the onboarding process referred to in these descriptions is also aspirational/hypothetical. At the time these core collective descriptions were developed the DNA builders envisioned an onboarding process that would include four distinct phases: (1) a set of self-directed preliminary activities and readings; (2) a reflective mutual discernment process to determine if the network is a good fit; (3) attendance at an intensive multi-day in-person onboarding training; (4) continuing enhancement trainings to deepen and expand understanding and embodiment of the network DNA.

Core Collectives

Power and Access Collective (partially centralized)

Purpose and Function

- To formulate and integrate a lens that supports the network's aims around racial healing, and which supports the integration of anti-racism and anti-oppression throughout the network, including both its centralized and decentralized elements. To help actualize the network's goals in relation to diversity and inclusion for the network's teams and collectives, including helping to ensure that people who come from marginalized communities and/or identities experience the network as a safe, caring and connecting community. In order to accomplish the above:

o   The collective will develop and facilitate a pre-onboarding diversity and inclusion audit for every prospective team and team-in-formation.

o   The collective will develop and facilitate a diversity and inclusion enhancement training for newly onboarded teams.

o   The collective will offer consultation and guidance to the Onboarding, Coaching, Conflict Engagement, and Network Feedback Collectives.

o   If situations arise when the recommended channels of communication in the network (i.e., a team communicating with their coach) would create a barrier to a member or team naming an issue or to their participation in the network, the Power and Access Collective would welcome hearing their feedback and will do what they can to support them to navigate the network system with appropriate care.

Centralized Functions

•   Two of the functions mentioned above are exclusive network roles held by this collective:

o   The collective will develop and facilitate the pre-onboarding diversity and inclusion audit for every prospective team and team-in-formation.

o   The collective will develop and facilitate the diversity and inclusion enhancement training included in phase four of the onboarding process.

Qualifications

- Have received positive feedback from BIPOC and other marginalized folks about their ability to offer empathy and other types of support

- Ability to see below the surface level of things in order to recognize patriarchal patterns and power dynamics, white supremacy, gaslighting, microaggressions, etc.

- Commitment to deep growth in their own practice of anti-racism and anti-oppression

- Ability to hold the needs of all involved with care, in a nonviolent spirit, in order to help build a call-in culture as opposed to a call-out culture

- Excellent communication skills

- Ability to self-regulate when triggered

Diversity and Inclusion

- The composition of the collective will reflect our network's commitment to fostering racial, gender identity and expression, religious, class and other forms of perspective diversity, as discussed in the fostering diversity section.

- At least half of the membership of this collective will be BIPOC.

- It is strongly recommended that at least half of the membership of this collective will be female-bodied and/or gender non-conforming.

Collective members commit to:

- Self-education around issues of power and privilege

- Meet regularly in order to support and learn from one another and to ensure teams receive similar levels of care

- Learn the beta test DNA thoroughly

- Embody the network principles and practices

Size of Group

- This collective consists of 4-6 members. The collective is encouraged to first select for the minimum number of 4 members. This is recommended so that as people emerge within the network with diverse perspectives and skills, some number of them can be added during the beta test period.

Term

- The collective is free to determine each member's term so long as (1) the terms are between one and three years, and (2) at least two members with at least one year experience in the main circle remain in it whenever someone completes their term and vacates the main circle. The intention here is to maintain staggered terms to allow for a healthy overlap of newcomers and those with more experience in the main circle of the collective.

- Members are free to serve multiple terms with the consent of the main circle of the collective.

Special Roles within the Collective

- Coordinator: the proverbial cat herder, in charge of scheduling and reminding collective members about upcoming meetings and supporting them to show up, stay on task, etc. The coordinator is selected by the collective sociocratically.

- Meeting facilitator

- Meeting note-taker

Determining Membership

- The initial formation of the collective will happen through an open sociocratic selection process (still to be determined). New members will be selected by the existing members of the collective using the sociocratic selection process.

Sub-circles

- Sub-circles may be formed at the discretion of the main circle

Onboarding Collective (centralized)

Purpose

- Develop and implement onboarding process for teams, including curriculum, trainers, and scheduling

- Mutual discernment with potential teams about fit in the network

- Transmitting the DNA and culture of the network

Qualifications

- Vocational match for teaching/learning and group skill development

- Ability and desire to build and maintain meaningful relationships at a distance

- Experienced trainer in key areas of focus for the network

- Know the handbook/DNA (be willing to learn it quickly)

- Experience designing accessible workshops and trainings

- Some members will need to be good with logistics and planning

- Availability for up to four hours a week during pre-launch phase (designing Phase 3 onboarding and updating other phases)

Diversity and Inclusion

- The composition of the collective will reflect our network's commitment to fostering racial, gender identity and expression, religious, class and other forms of perspective diversity, as discussed in the fostering diversity section.

Collective members commit to:

- Meet regularly in order to support and learn from one another.

- learn in depth the network DNA as described in the network handbook and additional onboarding materials

- Strive for deep embodiment of the network's principles and practices

- Stay informed about the resources available to teams (support offered by other collectives, resources named in the handbook, etc.). Share this information freely with teams.

- Clear and frequent communication with potential teams in phases 1-3 of the onboarding process

- Communicate as needed with the network feedback collective

- Communicate with the Coaching Collective to convey strengths, areas for growth, and other advice for supporting teams that trainers identified during phase 3 of the onboarding process.

- Develop and implement (or assign trainers to deliver) enhancement trainings.

Size of Group

- 4-8 members will be a part of the decision-making main circle, with at least 50% of members identified as BIPOC

- Additional trainers can be affiliated with the collective as a subcircle.

Term

- The collective is free to determine each member's term so long as (1) the terms are between one and three years, and (2) at least two members with at least one year experience in the main circle remain in it whenever someone completes their term and vacates the main circle. The intention here is to maintain staggered terms to allow for a healthy overlap of newcomers and those with more experience in the main circle of the collective.

- Members are free to serve multiple terms with the consent of the main circle of the collective.

Special Roles within the Collective

- Coordinator: the proverbial cat herder, in charge of scheduling and reminding collective members about upcoming meetings and supporting them to show up, stay on task, etc. The coordinator is selected by the collective sociocratically.

- Meeting facilitator

- Meeting note-taker

- Additional roles may be added, as needed, by the collective membership

Determining Membership

- At least 50% BIPOC

- Selection should prioritize gender diversity

- Geographic distribution of the members is important

- At least one member should have experience delivering transformational workshops in an online setting.

Additional Sub-circles

- Additional sub-circles may be formed at the discretion of the main circle. A subcircle of facilitators seems likely.

Coaching Collective (centralized)

Purpose and Function

- For each new team that fully onboards into the network, the weeks and months following the phase 3 onboarding will be the critical time for living into, learning, and deepening their commitments and fluency with network principles and practices (the DNA).

The role of the Coaching Collective is to accompany new teams through this process by offering practical support related to the continued learning and embodiment of the DNA, connection to network and other resources, and encouragement.

- While other coaching collectives may arise throughout the network, this Coaching Collective serves a unique role because of its centralized function. Members of this collective are matched with newly onboarded teams for a minimum of one year. (The process for matching coaches with teams will be determined by the collective.) This linkage between teams and this Coaching Collective will help ensure that all newly onboarded teams receive the same level of support as they learn the DNA and begin to live into it together.

- The collective is encouraged to inventory the individual gifts of its members, and to determine which coaches will be matched with which teams accordingly. Though each team will have one primary coach, the coaches may choose to work together by pooling their gifts to support teams.

- Each team and their coach will establish and maintain a regular rhythm of meetings. Each team will decide which member will serve as their coach's primary contact(s).

- During the first two months after a team onboards, each team's coach will facilitate a process to aid the team in identifying which of the network's recommended practices that the team wishes to engage in, in addition to the network's three core practices, as a means of deepening the team's collective embodiment of the network DNA. This process will also include the team deciding how long they wish to experiment with the recommended practices they choose, after which they will evaluate their experience with their coach.

- Two groups comprise the collective, a main circle of decision-makers for the collective and a subcircle of coaches. Members of the main circle can be part of the subcircle.

Qualifications

- Vocational match with the work of accompaniment and supportive learning

- Ability and desire to build and maintain meaningful relationships at a distance

- Attention to detail

- commitment to a thorough beta test of the DNA

- Has received feedback that you are skilled at helping people identify their needs and recognize their learning, at being prepared to try to understand how people are feeling and what they are struggling with, to help them go in the direction they need to go in, even when that is not necessarily the direction you might wish they would go. The coaching role is a support role, not a dictating or mandating role.

- If a person from a more privileged positionality, you have received feedback that you have the above skills in working with people who are marginalized.

- Ability to encourage vulnerable expression and to self-regulate so such expression is received with care.

- Good with interpersonal boundaries, deep listening, and not abusing vulnerable information.

Diversity and Inclusion

- The composition of the collective will reflect our network's commitment to fostering racial, gender identity and expression, religious, class and other forms of perspective diversity, as discussed in the fostering diversity section.

- The collective is encouraged to create an additional sub-circle of coaching apprentices, to help prepare them to meet the qualifications of membership in the collective.

Coaching Collective members commit to:

- Meet regularly in order to support and learn from one another and to ensure teams receive similar levels of coaching support.

- Learn in depth the network DNA as described in the network handbook and additional onboarding materials
- Strive for deep embodiment of the network's principles and practices

- Stay informed about the resources available to teams (support offered by other collectives, resources named in the handbook, etc.). Share this information freely with teams.

- Clear and frequent communication with other members of the collective and with one or more members of the team(s) they accompany for the duration of the coaching period.

- Communicate as needed with the network feedback collective

- Communicate with the Onboarding Collective to learn about strengths, areas for growth, and other advice for supporting teams that trainers identified during phase 3 of the onboarding process.

- Encourage and support teams to engage in essential enhancement trainings offered by the Onboarding Collective.

Additional commitments for members of the main circle (decision-makers) of the collective:

- To participate in additional meetings, likely once or twice per month.

Size of Group

- Main circle of the collective (decision makers): 4-6 members. The collective is encouraged to first select for the minimum number of four members. This is recommended so that as people emerge within the network with diverse perspectives and skills, some number of them can be added during the beta test period.

- Sub-circle of the collective (coaches): the collective will strive to have 1 qualified coach per team, but at least 1 for every two teams. The exact numbers won't be clear until we know how many teams have been onboarded during the beta-test year. Members of the main circle can be part of this sub-circle.

Term

- Main circle (decision-makers):

  o The main circle of the collective is free to determine each member's term so long as (1) the terms are between one and three years, and (2) at least two members with at least one year experience in the main circle remain in it whenever someone completes their term and vacates the main circle. The intention here is to maintain staggered terms to allow for a healthy overlap of newcomers and those with more experience in the main circle of the collective.

  o Members are free to serve multiple terms with the consent of the main circle of the collective.

- Sub-circle (coaches):

  o Coaches are assigned to teams by the main circle for a minimum of one year. Each coaching assignment is discrete. It is preferable that coaches hold one such assignment at any given time, but they may hold up to two. There is no time limit for coaches to remain part of the subcircle.

Special roles within the main circle of the collective

- Coordinator: the proverbial cat herder, in charge of scheduling and reminding collective members (for both the main and sub-circles) about upcoming meetings and supporting them to show up, stay on task, etc. The coordinator is selected by the main circle sociocratically.

- Meeting facilitator

- Meeting note-taker

Determining Membership

- Main circle (decision-makers):

- o   The initial formation of the collective will happen through an open sociocratic selection process (still to be determined). New members will be selected by the existing members of the collective using the sociocratic selection process.

- • Sub-circle (coaches):

  - o   Coaches are selected by the main circle using the sociocratic selection process.

Additional Sub-circles

- • Additional sub-circles may be formed at the discretion of the main circle.

Conflict Engagement Collective (partially centralized)

Purpose

- • To support healthy connection and collaboration in teams and collectives by offering:
  - o   Hands-on conflict facilitation, including mediation, restorative circle hosting, etc.

  - o   Facilitation of regular team Reflection Circles to support surfacing tensions and conflict within teams

  - o   Development and facilitation of the conflict engagement enhancement training included in phase four of the onboarding process.

  - o   Resources and additional training in various skills for and means of conflict engagement

  - o   Facilitation of the ultimate discernment process should member removal from the network be considered

Centralized functions

- • Three of the functions mentioned above are exclusive network roles held by this collective:

o Development and facilitation of the conflict engagement enhancement training included in phase four of the onboarding process

o Facilitation of quarterly team reflection circles to support individual and collective learning, connection, and conflict engagement

o Facilitation of the ultimate discernment process should member removal from the network be considered

Qualifications for main circle (decision-makers and ones taking the lead in fulfilling the above functional purpose of the collective)

- Foundational training and experience in facilitating conflict engagement and collective trauma healing

- Have a deep dedication to and have received feedback affirming their capacity to:

  o Welcome all voices and perspectives,

  o Empathize with and understand the needs of people with diverse perspectives, including those with which they disagree strongly

  o Recognize and own projections,

  o Transform blame and enemy images, and

  o Cultivate awareness of the impact of power and privilege on conflict

Qualifications for sub-circle (apprentice members who are in a learning process to become members of the main circle and who play an active support role in fulfilling the collective's purpose)

- Have begun foundational training in facilitating conflict engagement and collective trauma healing

- Have a deep dedication to:

  o Welcome all voices and perspectives,

  o Empathize with and understand the needs of people with
     diverse perspectives, including those with which they disagree
     strongly

  o Recognize and own projections,

  o Transform blame and enemy images, and

  o Cultivate awareness of the impact of power and privilege on
     conflict

Diversity and Inclusion

- Membership of the collective will reflect our network's commitment to fostering racial, gender identity and expression, religious,
  class, and other forms of diversity. The work of the collective dove-
  tails with both the conflict engagement system and the reflection
  circle process outlined in the network Handbook.

Both main circle members and apprentice members commit to:

- Do their own on-going inner work to heal and transform any inner
  blocks to welcoming and empathizing with diverse and extreme
  states and beliefs in others.

- Meet regularly in order to support and learn from one another
  and to ensure teams receive similar levels of conflict facilitation
  support.

- Learn the beta test DNA thoroughly

- Embody the network practices named in the DNA

- Encourage teams to engage in conflict engagement enhancement
  training offered by the Onboarding Collective.

Size of group

- This collective consists of 4-8 total members, including members
  of the main circle and apprentice members. The collective is

encouraged to first select for the minimum number of four members. This is recommended so that as people emerge within the network with diverse perspectives and skills, some number of them can be added during the beta test period.

Term

- Main circle:

  o The main circle of the collective is free to determine each member's term so long as (1) the terms are between one and three years, and (2) at least two members with at least one year experience in the main circle remain in it whenever someone completes their term and vacates the main circle. The intention here is to maintain staggered terms to allow for a healthy overlap of newcomers and those with more experience in the main circle of the collective.

  o Members are free to serve multiple terms with the consent of the main circle of the collective.

- Sub-circle (apprentices):

  o Apprentices will not serve as apprentices for a specific length of term. The collective anticipates that apprentices will be selected as members of the main circle after they have adequately fulfilled the corresponding qualifications. The period of time for that process will vary for each apprentice. The main circle will evaluate the progress of the apprentices on a regular basis.

Special roles within the collective

- Coordinator: the proverbial cat herder, in charge of scheduling and reminding collective members (for both the main and sub-circles) about upcoming meetings and supporting them to show up, stay on task, etc. The coordinator is selected by the main circle sociocratically.

- Meeting facilitator

- Meeting note-taker

Determining Membership

- Main circle

  - The initial formation of the collective will happen through an open sociocratic selection process (still to be determined). New members will be selected by the existing members of the collective using the sociocratic selection process.

- Sub-circle

  - Apprentices are selected by the main circle using the sociocratic selection process.

Additional Sub-circles

- Additional sub-circles may be formed at the discretion of the main circle.

Network Feedback Collective (centralized)

Purpose

- The Network Feedback Collective is charged with collecting, organizing, and disseminating feedback from network teams and collectives.

- Specifically, during the network's first year of beta-testing of the network DNA, this collective will gather information from the network's first cohort of teams, organize it, and pass it on to a yet-to-be-formed Network DNA Revision Collective (see below), which will integrate it into a second edition of this handbook.

- The Network Feedback Collective will work closely with the Power and Access Collective prior to passing on its report to the DNA Revision Collective, and will maintain close communication with other collectives so that incoming feedback from teams can improve and shape their work not only after but during the beta-test year.

Qualifications

- Excellent organizational skills, including ability to compile information with careful attention to accuracy and detail

- Excellent communication skills and note-taking

- Objectivity

- Experience preparing and presenting lengthy, multi-layered reports or documents

Diversity and Inclusion

- The composition of the collective will reflect our network's commitment to fostering racial, gender identity and expression, religious, class and other forms of perspective diversity, as discussed in the fostering diversity section.

Collective members commit to:

- Learn in depth the network DNA as described in the network handbook and additional onboarding materials

- Being easily accessible to receive feedback from all corners of the network

- Working closely with the Coaching Collective to establish a regular rhythm of receiving feedback from all teams in the network

- Documenting and transmitting feedback as accurately and objectively as possible

- Directing network members to the Coaching Collective for support in addressing the concerns they raise. If concerns raised are about the Coaching Collective, encouraging network members to reach out to the Conflict Engagement Collective for help

- Integrating the advice and guidance of the Power and Access Collective prior to submitting their beta-test year-end report to the DNA Revision Collective

Size of Group

- This collective consists of 3-5 members. The collective is encouraged to first select for the minimum number of 3 members. This is recommended so that as people emerge within the network with diverse perspectives and skills, some number of them can be added during the beta test period.

Term

- The collective is free to determine each member's term so long as (1) the terms are between one and two years, and (2) at least one member holds a two year term. The network anticipates that this collective will continue to be essential after the beta-test year, and that a rhythm will be established for DNA revision moving forward. Having at least one collective member continue through the second year will allow for a healthy overlap with newcomers to the collective.

Special Roles within the Collective

- Coordinator: the proverbial cat herder, in charge of scheduling and reminding collective members about upcoming meetings and supporting them to show up, stay on task, etc. The coordinator is selected by the collective sociocratically.

- Meeting facilitator

- Meeting note-taker

Determining Membership

- The initial formation of the collective will happen through an open sociocratic selection process (still to be determined). New members will be selected by the existing members of the collective using the sociocratic selection process.

Sub-circles

- Sub-circles may be formed at the discretion of the main circle.

Internal Reparations Collective (not centralized)

Because this collective does not have a centralized function beyond the participation of its representative on the Stewardship Circle, a minimum amount of structure was built into it, in order to allow the collective itself to determine many of its own policies and norms.

Purpose

- To serve teams and collectives in the network by facilitating internal reparations redistribution (i.e., the moving of resources from white people in and potentially beyond the network to BIPOC people in the network or BIPOC folks who wish to participate in network-related activities).

- This collective is fully decentralized, which means that some teams and collectives may choose to handle their internal reparations commitments without interacting with the collective.

- Note: East Point Peace Academy (EPPA) has offered to receive/hold funds and cut checks on behalf of the Internal Reparations Collective. If the Internal Reparations Collective accepts this offer, EPPA agrees that none of their staff will serve on the collective and that EPPA will have no role in determining where funds are distributed.

Qualifications

- Especially strong vocational match with the network's reparations approach, practically and philosophically

- Ability and desire to build and maintain meaningful relationships at a distance

- Attention to detail, especially tracking financial disbursements

- Non-judgmental presence

- High degree of awareness and understanding of the dynamics of power and privilege

Diversity and Inclusion

- As with all collectives, the composition of the Internal Reparations Collective will reflect our network's commitment to fostering racial, gender identity and expression, religious, class and other forms of perspective diversity, as discussed in the fostering diversity section.

- It is strongly recommended that at least half of the membership of this collective will be BIPOC people.

- It is strongly recommended that at least half of the membership of this collective will be female-bodied and/or gender non-conforming.

Size of Group

- The recommendation of the home stretch team is 3-6 members.

Once the collective has at least 3 members, it will determine its own policies regarding membership expectations, roles, terms, membership, and the potential formation of sub-circles within the collective.

DNA Revision Collective (centralized)

Purpose

- To review the feedback received by the Network Feedback Collective over the network's beta-testing year, and incorporate that feedback into a second edition of the handbook.

Qualifications

- Team player, good at collaboration, and open to hearing and seeking to understand diverse perspectives, including those with which they disagree

- Must have ample time over the course of time period without a clear endpoint

- At least a few members of the collective must be a strong vocational match for the hands-on writing and editing demands of a lengthy, multilayered writing project

Diversity and Inclusion

- The composition of the collective will reflect our network's commitment to fostering racial, gender identity and expression, religious, class and other forms of perspective diversity, as discussed in the fostering diversity section.

- It is strongly recommended that at least half of the membership of this collective will be BIPOC.
- It is strongly recommended that at least half of the membership of this collective will be female-bodied and/or gender non-conforming.

- It is strongly recommended that the collective has at least one member from each region where onboarded teams are located.

Collective members commit to:

- See the second edition of the handbook through to the end

- Carefully review the report of the Network Feedback Collective and to work closely with that collective to understand as best as possible the learning that happened during the beta-test year

- Diligent adherence to the network's principles and practices over the course of the collective's work together, with special emphasis on decision-making, giving and receiving feedback, and conflict engagement practices

Size of group

- Six

Term

- Until the second edition of the Handbook is completed.

Special Roles within the Collective

- Coordinator: the proverbial cat herder, in charge of scheduling and reminding collective members about upcoming meetings and supporting them to show up, stay on task, etc. The coordinator is selected by the collective sociocratically.

- Meeting facilitator

- Meeting note-taker

Sub-Circles

- Sub-circles may be established at the discretion of the main circle

Stewardship Circle (centralized)

Purpose

- The Stewardship Circle serves as the hub for information sharing and cross-fertilization between the network's Core Collectives. The linkages between these collectives are vital to the healthy flow of information which impacts the entire network's ability to learn and grow.

Membership

- Each of the six Core Collectives (Power and Access, Onboarding, Coaching, Conflict Engagement, Network Feedback, and Internal Reparations) will appoint a representative to the Stewardship Circle. Once the DNA Revision Collective is formed, a representative from that Collective will also join the Stewardship Circle making the total membership seven people.

Meeting Rhythm

- The Stewardship Circle meets on a monthly basis; and additionally, as needed.

Decision-Making and Meeting Format Resources

The following handouts from Sociocracy for All[31] give a taste of some of the decision-making and meeting format elements that will be explored during the onboarding process (still to be developed).

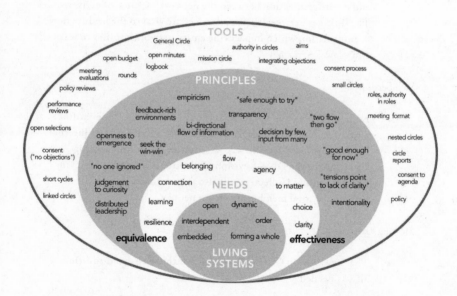

---

31. https://www.sociocracyforall.org/

Meeting format IN SOCIOCRACY

Check-in

"How are you entering this meeting?"

"Let's make everything is taken care of before we start on our agenda items."

Agenda

"Let me describe the agenda..."
"Are there any additions to the agenda?"
"Are there any objections to the agenda?"

Topics

Decision: *"Let's see if we can make a decision on..."*
Exploration: *"We will gather some ideas/feedback on..."*
Report: *"Let's make sure we all know what's happening on..."*

Backlog

"What from today's meeting needs to go on the backlog?"
(term ends - roles/policy;follow-up topics /new items

Evaluation

"How are you leaving this meeting?"
"How could we improve content, process, interpersonal dynamics?"

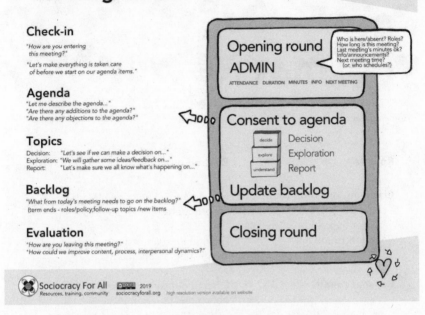

Sociocracy For All
Resources, training, community   2019   sociocracyforall.org   high resolution version available on website

---

SOCIOCRATIC MEETING FORMATS AND DECISION-MAKING

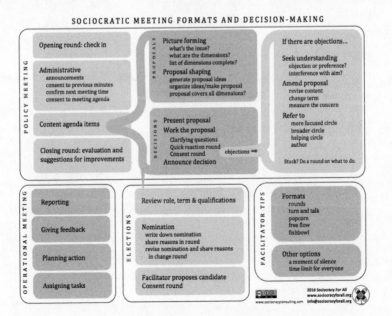

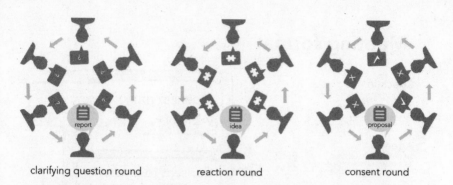

clarifying question round   reaction round   consent round

Rounds	Desired outcome
Clarifying question round	Making sure everyone understands a report, a proposal or an idea.
Reaction round	Giving feedback, exploring ideas, suggesting amendments.
Consent round	Finding out whether there are objections to a proposal.

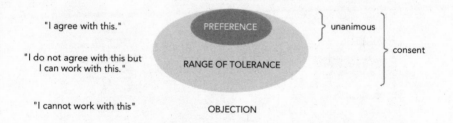

"I agree with this."

"I do not agree with this but I can work with this."

"I cannot work with this"

PREFERENCE

RANGE OF TOLERANCE

OBJECTION

} unanimous

} consent

Selection process

UNDERSTAND	EXPLORE	DECIDE
Understand role *"What is the role description?"*	**Nominations** Write down nominations	**Propose candidate** Candidate, term, reasons
Explore qualifications *"What qualities would you like to see in this role?"*	**Nomination round** *"Who did you nominate and why?"*	**Consent round** *"Do you consent to this candidate filling the role?"*
Synthesize Consent to list of qualifications	**Change round** *"Do you change your nomination and why (not)?"*	**Output decision** Publish decision

Resource Flow and Cost-Sharing for Events

There are a few different ways that network teams have experimented with sharing information about the cost of an event, and the process of transparently collectivizing expenses. Below are two examples you are welcome to experiment with.

Model One

One model is to list all of the different needs/expenses separately on a large sheet of paper, similar to the diagram on the adjacent page. The invitation is for event participants to give any amount of money and designate their gift to a specific need/expense. They are also welcome to give to multiple areas.

With each gift, the Money Steward would update the sheet, listing the new gift and the updated goal for that area.

Displaying the individual gift amounts achieves transparency, allows others to check your math, and provides a clear picture of how many people are participating and at what levels.

How to read this chart: In the section for internal reparations, the flow of funds began with someone giving $25 before any needs were known (so the initial "current need" was -$25). Next, someone requested $50 from the internal reparations pool, bringing the new "current need" to $25. Then, someone requested $72 from the internal reparations pool, bringing the "current need" to $97. Finally, someone gave $95 toward internal reparations, bringing the "current need" figure to $2.

Model Two

Another way to offer this is to share with the participants all of the financial needs in a similar fashion, but also provide them with the total sum of all the expenses/needs. Participants are then asked to give to one shared fund, rather than giving to a specific cost or expense.

At the end of the gathering, the organizers can come together and decide how to share the resources that have come in. If the resources that come in do not meet the total goal, the organizers can decide how to split the difference. If it exceeds the goal, they can decide how to share the abundance. Either way, the participants should be informed of the final breakdown.

To contribute or receive support talk to NAME OF MONEY STEWARD(S)! Gifts can be in the form of: cash, checks made out to NAME OF MONEY STEWARD(S), by Venmo to @ACCOUNTNAME, or by Paypal to @ACCOUNTNAME Please help us celebrate other gifts (food, songleading, rideshare, and more!) by recording them on this page!	<u>Food</u> ($350 spent, estimated $100 more) <u>Remaining need</u> = ~~$450~~ ~~$375~~ $200 <u>$ Gifts</u>: - $75 remaining from previous gathering -$175 gift <u>Other Gifts</u>: - 5 lb bag of carrots - homemade hummus
External reparations (e.g. donation to local indigenous-led land rematriation effort) <u>Goal</u> = $170 <u>Remaining need</u> = ~~$155~~ $90 <u>$ Gifts</u>: - $15 - $65	<u>Internal reparations</u> (support for time to be here, travel, other expenses) <u>Current need</u> = "$ Gifts out" minus "$ Gifts in" = ~~(-$25)~~ ~~$25~~ ~~$97~~ $2 **$ Gifts in:** / **$ Gifts out:** - $25 / - $50 - $95 / - $72 <u>Other Gifts</u>: - 10 hours of childcare from network member
<u>Support for guest speakers/facilitators</u> (goal is 3 people, $100 each) <u>Remaining need</u>: ~~$300~~ ~~$275~~ $195 <u>$ Gifts</u>: - $25 - $80	<u>Contribution to the space/room rental</u> (goal= $100) <u>Remaining need</u> = ~~$80~~ $75 <u>$ Gifts</u>: $20 $5
Extra funds in space/food/internal reparations categories will be saved for our next gathering. Extra funds in external reparations/support for guests will go to them.	

Principles of Gift Economics

From East Point Peace Academy

Generosity

Pure generosity means giving without any expectation of some reward or exchange. The giving that happens is not part of a transaction; rather, it is part of the transformation of our culture and relationships. We give, because the act of giving benefits and brings joy to both the giver and the recipient. In this way, all of our programs are offered as a gift, regardless of a participant's ability to pay.

In a market economy, exchanges are transactional. In the Gift Economy, exchanges are transformational because the gift is made out of a desire to support others.

Access

We are committed to practices—financial and otherwise—that allow for the full participation of as many people as possible.

In the market economy, goods and services are assigned a monetary value, which not only diminishes the true value of our gifts, but also creates a barrier to access. By acknowledging the priceless nature of our gifts, we are able to create more access.

Interdependence

Unlike the market economy which encourages autonomy and self-reliance, the Gift system is a reciprocal system that acknowledges the interdependence of all life— what affects one directly affects all indirectly. A Gift system functions to the extent that people give in support of one another. The responsibility to meet our needs is held collectively, as opposed to each individual being mandated to pay some set amount.

Because giving in a market system is transactional and motivated by a desire to receive something (either payment or a particular good/service), the exchange benefits those directly involved. In a Gift system, because giving is voluntary and made out of the desire to support others in a "pay-it-forward" approach, that gift will go on to support those you may never meet.

Intentionality

Rather than living with an assumption that constant growth is always positive, we make our decisions with careful intention. As Gandhi once said, the world has enough for "everyone's needs, and no one's greed." This means having conversations about how we want to relate to money: how much we need, who we take money from, what kind of growth we want, etc.

In a market economy, the constant growth mentality of "bigger is always better" is pervasive, even in nonprofits. We take a different approach, and do not always assume that having more funds and growing larger as an organization is better.

Equity

We acknowledge that a cookie-cutter, one-size-fits-all approach to economics can perpetuate disparity. We work to honor the story, ability and capacity of each person in the room in order to create equity. The Gift system thrives when those who have the capacity to give more than their "fair market share" give more than those with less financial capacity.

The market economy conditions us to constantly be on the lookout for the "best bargain," to pay as little as we can and to get the most "bang for our buck." This approach rarely meets the needs of all parties. The Gift system looks at the ability of all parties, and inspires us to develop our collective capacity to meet everyone's needs.

Transparency

We work to counter a culture of security and secrecy with trust and transparency. In order to empower each person to make decisions that are right for them, we are committed to a culture of radical financial transparency.

Unlike a market economy where personal and organizational finances are held as tightly guarded secrets, we share our financial information with our community on a regular basis.

Faith

Rather than relying on strategic plans and fundraising strategies, we rely on relationships and a faith that if our work is meant to exist in the world, our community will come together to sustain it. Rather than living in a scarcity model and pouring resources into fundraising, we try to live into the abundance of our world and steer our resources toward the work we're most called to do.

These principles of the Gift Economy were originally developed and shared by the East Bay Meditation Center, and adapted by
East Point Peace Academy.
See www.eastpointpeace.org/gifteconomics for more.

Five Economies for Breaking Free from Colonial Capitalism

A Working Document from the Possibility Alliance

"So if you are, in contrast, really depending on the empire, depending on a system that hates you, for all your basic systems, you're not going to be able to really resist that system because you're intertwined with its success."

~ Leah Penniman, *Soul Fire Farm* ~

ECO-nomy ("home" + "management"): Economy means management of home. How we organize our relationships in a place, ideally, to take care of the place and each other. But "management of home." can be good or bad, depending on how you do it and to what ends. The purpose of our economy could be turning land, life and labor into property for a few, or returning land, life and labor into a balanced web of stable relationships.

> Economy does not mean money, or exchange
> or financial markets, or trading or
> Gross Domestic Product. These are simply
> elements or tools of specific economies.
> Economies ("how we manage our home") can
> be measured in many ways: How healthy are
> the soil, people, water, animals? How
> much wealth is generated? Who owns the
> wealth? What even constitutes wealth?
> Is it money? Well-being? Happiness?
>
> - Movement Generation's zine,
> **_From Banks and Tanks to Cooperation
> and Caring_**

The Five Economies for Breaking Free from Colonial Capitalism work in synergy to help us escape the capitalistic domination system. Remove one of these economies and the effectiveness is weakened. Each economy feeds the other. For example, when we practice Relational Economy, we build community which gives us more support for creative replacement of certain ways we meet our needs, which is Reduction/Contentment economy. This leads to having extra and lets us join the Gift Economy.

Is there another economy that would strengthen and complement these five?

1. **Relational Economy**. How many reciprocal relationships can you create/have?

    Human togetherness. The more we tie in with each other, the less we need capitalistic systems. E.g.: sharing space, working on projects together, being each other's healers, therapists, carpenters, etc. Sharing, taking on each other's debt, creating belonging.

    Nature/species/ecosystem community. The more we tie in with nature, the less we need things from the extraction/destruction economy. E.g.: food from the land, fire for heat, water from rain catchment, herbs for medicine, homes built out of local materials. Belonging to the world.

2. **Reduction/Contentment Economy**. How many of your needs can you fulfill on your heart's terms?

Remove (or do without). Learn to stop consuming: remove things you do not need in order to live. Things humans thrived without for millions of years: movies, restaurants, exotic vacations, professional sports, luxury cash crops: coffee, chocolate, etc., TV, plastic, anything your distant ancestors thrived without. If a real need is missing after the removal (i.e., movies fill a real need for entertainment/play) replace it on your heart's terms.

Replace on your heart's terms. Replace the needs industrial domination economies have been filling. E.g.: stop going to movies, but go to local theater. Stop eating chocolate but make local strawberry rhubarb pies. Stop going to restaurants but rotate going "out to eat" at friends' homes or the park. Replacement economics requires community and creativity.

3. **Gift Economy**. Giving and receiving are linked and must keep occurring for the gift to gain momentum.

Giving: What do you have lots of? Time, skills, empathy, money, land, etc.? Begin to gift it. Pass it on so it can flow and not be withheld. Kahlil Gibran writes: "To withhold is to perish." This helps us remember our interdependence. Can you run your organization, cottage industry, or healing practice in the gift economy? Give it a try. Ask your community what it needs.

Receiving: Receiving can often be more difficult than giving. Can you ask your community for what you need? It takes vulnerability to be a receiver. This creates bonds of positive obligation and reciprocity. We belong and are accountable to each other. This also weakens the spell of separation.

4. **Give Back Economy**. The Give Back Economy flows to all current and historically oppressed communities. Those forcefully cut out of colonial-capitalism.

Much has been stolen historically and much is being stolen at this very moment: land, time, lives, families, dignity, freedom, natural resources. For the other four economies to work, what can be returned must be returned. Otherwise there is a deep imbalance in the whole. Give back what you can: time, land, goods, money, services, etc. to these communities. With this you tangibly and respectfully acknowledge the original trauma wounds, also known as legacy trauma, of genocide against the original people of this land, and the kidnapping, murder, and slavery of Africans. It is simple. Give back so that these marginalized communities have much needed resources.

5. **Gratitude and Mindfulness Economy**. The more grateful and mindful we are, the less we "need."

The more we can feel gratitude for all we have been given: life, air, water, friends, sunsets, our bodies and senses, etc., the less our manufactured desire to consume is activated. By practicing gratitude, we can see the needs that are being fulfilled outside of domination capitalism. The more we practice mindfulness and stay in the moment, the more we belong to ourselves, the more we belong to each other and the world. Mindfulness reduces our addiction to consumption, distraction, and "new experiences." We develop gratitude and mindfulness as an antidote to extraction and consumption.

The Synergy of the 5 Economies

Participating in the Give Back Economy can build relationships, thus making the Relational Economy more activated. The deepening of diverse relationships can lead to the need to remove things that are oppressing these communities. Things linked, for example, to the corporations oppressing or extracting from them. The Mindfulness/Gratitude Economy can make you feel less fearful and scarcity-minded, leading you to join in more fully to the Gift, Give Back, Relational or Reduction economies. The linkages go on and on between the five economies. When communities practice Replacement Economics they naturally start practicing Relational Economics. This also leads to deeper connection to the natural world, which is part of the Relational Economy (growing food, hiking, eating in parks etc.) This also leads to Gift Economics, people sharing time, ideas, resources and much more to make Replacement Economics work.

In one outing you could activate all five economies. For example, instead of going to a Hollywood movie you go to the local theater [2] operated by a BIPOC-led theater company. You pay for tickets and give a donation [4]. As a gift, you bring some youth who could not afford tickets [3]. You also bring some fruit you grew to share with other members of the audience [1]. Afterward, you walk home doing a walking meditation [5].

Transcription of original draft: https://bit.ly/3DNQngz

Community Welcome Statement

This is a sample welcome statement, borrowed from friends at Canticle Farm, that many teams in the network have used to start gatherings and events . You can invite all participants to join in voicing the "WELCOME" after each statement. Adjust the land acknowledgement in the 8th paragraph for your location.

All beings that inhabit Earth, human or otherwise: the two-legged, the four-legged, winged and finned, those that walk, fly, and crawl above the ground and below, in air and water. We say, "WELCOME."

People on all parts of the continuum of gender identity and sexual expression. Lesbian, gay, bisexual, heterosexual, transgender, gender fluid and non-binary, gender queer and two spirit people, all other queer folks; the sexually active and the celibate, and everyone for whom these labels don't apply. We say, "WELCOME."

People of African descent, of Asian descent, of European descent, of First Nations descent in this land and abroad; people of mixed and multiple descents, and all of the languages spoken here. We say, "WELCOME."

Your bodies and bodies of all shapes and sizes, of all abilities and challenges. Those living with a chronic medical condition, visible or invisible. We say, "WELCOME."

People of all ages, those about to be born, the voices of small children. All elder bodies, all pregnant bodies, all menstruating bodies and those who are currently bleeding; your ceremony is honored here. We say, "WELCOME."

People who identify as activists and those who don't. Mystics, believers, non-believers, seekers of all kinds. Those who practice the Old Ways, all ancient and enduring Earth-honoring traditions, witches, pagans, pantheists, and wild creatures. Those who support us to be here. We say, "WELCOME."

Your emotions: joy, fear, grief, contentment, disappointment, surprise, outrage, anger and all else that flows through you. We say, "WELCOME."

Your families, genetic and otherwise. Those dear to us who have died. Our ancestors and the future ones. The ancestors who lived in this land in this place where these buildings are now: Huichin (Hoo-chin) village of the Chochenyo Ohlone (Cho-chen-yo O-lone-ee) people. We honor you through this work that we are undertaking. We say, "WELCOME."

We welcome all the plants, the green beings, the grasses and herbs, the flowers, cacti, shrubs and the tall trees from all places: redwood, oak, pine, cedar, willow, cypress and yew; the trees from the rainforests and swamps, the river bottoms and deserts; and also your wonderful companions, the mushrooms, the fungi that enrich and hold your soil and decompose your bodies to enhance Earth. We say, "WELCOME."

All non-material beings of this place and all places: beings of the wind, the forest, the desert, the ocean, as well as of this particular place, whether it is still intact and wild, or domesticated and paved over. We welcome you with the names the people native to this place gave you, and with the names by which you know yourselves. We say, "WELCOME."

Created/adapted in partnership at Canticle Farm. Always a work in progress. Updated as of 9/18. Original by Training for Change: www.trainingforchange.org/training_ tools/diversity-welcome/

Principles of Environmental Justice

Drafted and adopted by the delegates to the First National People of Color Environmental Leadership Summit held on October 24-27, 1991, in Washington, DC.

WE, THE PEOPLE OF COLOR, gathered together at this multinational People of Color Environmental Leadership Summit, to begin to build a national and international movement of all peoples of color to fight the destruction and taking

of our lands and communities, do hereby re-establish our spiritual interdependence
to the sacredness of our Mother Earth; to respect and celebrate each of our cultures,
languages and beliefs about the natural world and our roles in healing ourselves;
to ensure environmental justice; to promote economic alternatives which would
contribute to the development of environmentally safe livelihoods; and, to secure
our political, economic and cultural liberation that has been denied for over 500
years of colonization and oppression, resulting in the poisoning of our communities
and land and the genocide of our peoples, do affirm and adopt these Principles of
Environmental Justice:

1. Environmental Justice affirms the sacredness of Mother Earth,
   ecological unity and the interdependence of all species, and the
   right to be free from ecological destruction.

2. Environmental Justice demands that public policy be based on
   mutual respect and justice for all peoples, free from any form of
   discrimination or bias.

3. Environmental Justice mandates the right to ethical, balanced and
   responsible uses of land and renewable resources in the interest of
   a sustainable planet for humans and other living things.

4. Environmental Justice calls for universal protection from nuclear
   testing, extraction, production and disposal of toxic/hazardous
   wastes and poisons and nuclear testing that threaten the
   fundamental right to clean air, land, water, and food.

5. Environmental Justice affirms the fundamental right to political,
   economic, cultural and environmental self-determination of all
   peoples.

6. Environmental Justice demands the cessation of the production
   of all toxins, hazardous wastes, and radioactive materials, and
   that all past and current producers be held strictly accountable to
   the people for detoxification and the containment at the point of
   production.

7. Environmental Justice demands the right to participate as
   equal partners at every level of decision-making, including
   needs assessment, planning, implementation, enforcement and
   evaluation.

8. Environmental Justice affirms the right of all workers to a safe and healthy work environment without being forced to choose between an unsafe livelihood and unemployment. It also affirms the right of those who work at home to be free from environmental hazards.

9. Environmental Justice protects the right of victims of environmental injustice to receive full compensation and reparations for damages as well as quality health care.

10. Environmental Justice considers governmental acts of environmental injustice a violation of international law, the Universal Declaration of Human Rights, and the United Nations Convention on Genocide.

11. Environmental Justice must recognize a special legal and natural relationship of Native Peoples to the U.S. government through treaties, agreements, compacts, and covenants affirming sovereignty and self-determination.

12. Environmental Justice affirms the need for urban and rural ecological policies to clean up and rebuild our cities and rural areas in balance with nature, honoring the cultural integrity of all our communities, and providing fair access for all to the full range of resources.

13. Environmental Justice calls for the strict enforcement of principles of informed consent, and a halt to the testing of experimental reproductive and medical procedures and vaccinations on people of color.

14. Environmental Justice opposes the destructive operations of multinational corporations.

15. Environmental Justice opposes military occupation, repression and exploitation of lands, peoples and cultures, and other life forms.

16. Environmental Justice calls for the education of present and future generations which emphasizes social and environmental issues, based on our experience and an appreciation of our diverse cultural perspectives.

17. Environmental Justice requires that we, as individuals, make personal and consumer choices to consume as little of Mother Earth's resources and to produce as little waste as possible; and make the conscious decision to challenge and reprioritize our lifestyles to ensure the health of the natural world for present and future generations.

Rupa Marya on Colonization

An excerpt of her keynote address at the 2018 National Bioneers Conference [32]

To understand the root causes of the pathologies we see today which impact all of us but affect Brown, Black and Poor people more intensely, we have to examine the foundations of this society which began with COLONIZATION.

To me, to be colonized means to be disconnected and disintegrated— from our ancestry, from the earth, from our indigeneity, our earth-connected selves. We all come from earth-connected people, people who once lived in deep connection to the rhythms of nature. I believe it is not a coincidence that the colonization of this land happened at the same time that Europeans were burning hundreds of thousands of witches, those women who carried the traditional indigenous knowledge of the tribes of Europe.

Colonization was the way the extractive economic system of Capitalism came to this land, supported by systems of supremacy and domination which are a necessary part to keep wealth and power accumulated in the hands of the colonizers and ultimately their financiers.

In what is now known as the US, this system of supremacy is expressed in many ways with many outcomes but we will focus on specific ones for the sake of time. First white supremacy, which created a framework that legitimized slavery and genocide. Slavery created cheap labor which is necessary for a functioning capitalist system. And genocide created unlimited access to resources, in the form of land, animal parts, minerals and raw materials which are also necessary for a functioning

---

32. Marya, Rupa. "Health and Justice: The Path of Liberation through Medicine." https://bit.ly/3LFBuj5.

capitalist economy. And as capitalism functions, it further entrenches systems of supremacy.

We all know that white supremacy looks like scary people with swastikas in hoods. But it can also look like any place where there's an abundance of white people in exclusive contexts, where power and access is not readily ceded to others.

There's white supremacy and then there's male supremacy, aka patriarchy, which leads to the invisibilizing of women's labor (you know, like creating the entire human race out of our bodies) or in this context, reproducing the work force and suppressing our wages, which further supports capitalism. Patriarchy also leads to femicide, domestic violence and child abuse, which we see across all groups here.

We also see human supremacy, where people feel superior to the rest of living entities, thereby subjecting living soils, seeds, animals, plants and water to horrific treatment in the name of exploiting resources, which in turn feeds the capitalist need for ever-increasing profits.

While this wheel of domination, exploitation, generation and seques- tration of wealth continues, we experience as a byproduct and common pathway, TRAUMA, and many studies have shown us that chronic stress and trauma create chronic inflammation.

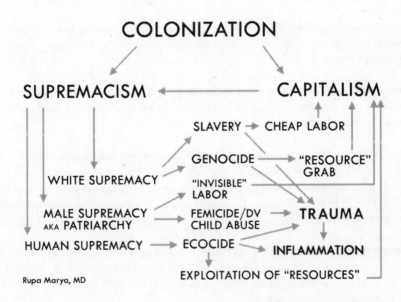

Rupa Marya, MD

Five Opportunities for Healing and Making Room for Growth

**Resmaa Menakem, from the Afterword
to _My Grandmother's Hands_[33]**

The healing of trauma, and creating room for growth in the nervous systems of our children and other human beings, does not only happen in therapists' offices. Our everyday lives present us with endless opportunities to heal—through the things we say and do, the harmful things we are able to not say and do, and the ways in which we treat ourselves and others. We all have the capacity to heal—and to create room for others to heal. Our relationships, communities, and circumstances all call us into this healing.

Life offers us five types of such opportunities. If you're fortunate, all five may be open to you. Most of us can practice at least the first three. Since you're reading these words, you're already practicing the first.

Opportunity #1: Healing on your own. You can read (and reread) this book and follow its guidance. More important, you can regularly practice some of the activities presented in this book—especially the five anchors in Chapter Twelve.

Opportunity #2: Healing with another trusted, caring person. This might be a friend, a partner, or a family member. You can talk with them about your experiences, your concerns, your family and ancestors, and/or your hopes for the future. They can listen and support you as you metabolize some of your trauma and move through it. You might listen and support them in their own healing, as well.

Opportunity #3: Healing in community. With other people you know and care about, you can practice some of the shared healing practices in this book. You might also ask a trusted community figure—such as an elder, a spiritual leader, or a community activist—to listen, support you, and offer their guidance.

---

33 . _My Grandmother's Hands: Racialized Trauma and the Pathway to Mending Our Hearts and Bodies_, Central Recovery Press, 2017.

Opportunity #4: Healing with the help of a body-focused healing professional. This might be a craniosacral healer, a massage therapist, an energy worker (such as a Reiki practitioner), an osteopath, a homeopath, or an acupuncturist.

Opportunity #5: Healing with the help of a trauma therapist. This is the deepest and most life-changing form of healing. Trauma therapists have tools and skills that most other therapists do not. Usually these include some combination of Somatic Experiencing (SE), Sensorimotor Psychotherapy (SP), Eye Movement Desensitization and Reprocessing (EMDR), neurofeedback, and/or emotion-focused therapy (also known as process-experiential therapy). You can find a good list of trauma therapists on the website of the Somatic Experiencing Trauma Institute at https://traumahealing.org/.

The more opportunities you practice, the better. But each one is important—and each can help mend your trauma, create more room for future generations, and heal the world.

For Starting/ Grounding Meetings and Gatherings

Deeply aware of the humbling enormity of the crises humanity is facing and our own imperfections, we are nonetheless determined to act. As we move forward, we pledge to listen, learn, experiment, and grow; to make our mistakes, adapt, and try, try again.

We are one element in an expansive movement ecosystem, a "movement of movements," each part of which is essential. Within this movement ecosystem, our network is called to two inseparable core commitments:

To contribute to racial healing and reconciliation by making and facilitating concrete acts of reparations

To honor, uplift, and defend life through bold civil disobedience and creative initiative to address racial injustice and the climate emergency.

We are not here to win.
We are here to be our true selves and to serve life.

Additional Resources

Climate Crisis

Articles:
- The Guardian's Climate Crisis section: https://bit.ly/3r5Lp9C
- Truthout's Climate Disruption Dispatches: https://bit.ly/3x5abb2

Books:
- *The End of Ice: Bearing Witness and Finding Meaning in the Path of Climate Disruption* by Dahr Jamail
- *This Changes Everything: Capitalism vs. the Climate* by Naomi Klein
- *The Sixth Extinction: An Unnatural History* by Elizabeth Kolbert
- *The End of Nature* by Bill BcKibben
- *The Weather Makers: How Man Is Changing the Climate and What It Means for Life on Earth* by Tim Flannery

Films:
- Thank You For the Rain: https://bit.ly/3v2gpsn
- The Condor and the Eagle: https://bit.ly/3Kj4TiL
- Cooked: Survival By Zip Code: https://to.pbs.org/3uent5M
- Disobedience: https://bit.ly/3xaVO7Q

Reports:
- Fourth National Climate Assessment, U.S. Global Change Research Program: https://bit.ly/360jFZ1
- Global Warming of 1.5 °C (summary), The Intergovernmental Panel on Climate Change: https://bit.ly/2SBi7Sl

Videos:
- Wake Up, Freak Out – Then Get a Grip: https://bit.ly/37ptdAY
- Climate Crisis Myths: Science, Racism, Ethics & Action by Kritee (Kanko): https://bit.ly/3drdS34

Websites:
- The Intergovernmental Panel on Climate Change: https://www.ipcc.ch
- United Nations: Climate Action: https://bit.ly/3KlEMaQ

The Inseparability of Racial Justice and Climate Justice

Articles:

- "Racism is Killing the Planet" by Hop Hopkins: https://bit.ly/3hh0krL
- "Let Them Drown: The Violence of Othering in a Warming World" by Naomi Klein: https://bit.ly/3h4zrZ8
- "White Supremacy = Mother of Climate Crisis" by Kritee (Kanko): https://bit.ly/35YBuaW
- "People of Color Experience Climate Grief More Deeply Than White People" by Nylah Burton: https://bit.ly/3dnUJ1K
- "Unequal Impact: The Deep Links Between Racism and Climate Change" by Beth Gardiner: https://bit.ly/3dn1G3d
- "Why Is Climate Change a Racial Justice Issue?" by Joe McCarthy: https://bit.ly/2UftUWH
- "Black Lives Matter: The Link Between Climate Change and Racial Justice" by Adelle Thomas & Rueanna Haynes: https://bit.ly/3w7SJkN

Books:

- *The Wrong Complexion for Protection* by Beverly Wright and Robert Bullard
- *Farming While Black: Soul Fire Farm's Practical Guide to Liberation on the Land* by Leah Penniman
- *The Indigenous Fight for Environmental Justice: from Colonization to Standing Rock* by Dina Gilio-Whitaker
- *A Terrible Thing to Waste: Environmental Racism and Its Assault on the American Mind* by Harriet A. Washington

Reparations and Atonement

Articles:

- "The Case for Reparations" by Ta-Nehisi Coates: https://bit.ly/3AezskK
- "This Country Needs a Truth and Reconciliation Process on Violence Against African Americans—Right Now" by Fania Davis: https://bit.ly/3w2yyoh
- "UN Human Rights Chief Calls for Reparations Over Racism" by BBC: https://bbc.in/3x9NEdc

- "The Forty Acres Documents: An Introduction" by Amilcar Shabazz: https://bit.ly/2UeuaFn
- "The Demon in Darren Wilson's Head" by Thandeka: https://bit.ly/2Tnh2Oa
- "DIY Reparations: How I Can Offer Reparations in Direct Proportion to My White Privilege" by Chris Moore-Backman: https://bit.ly/2Thyfsk

Audio:
- Reparations: From Conversation to ACTION! webinar by Fellowship of Reconciliation: https://bit.ly/2UUZoSF

Books:
- *Buffalo Shout, Salmon Cry: Conversations on Creation, Land Justice, and Life Together* by Steve Heinrichs
- *Classified: How to Stop Hiding your Privilege and Use it for Social Change* by Karen Pittelman & Resource Generation
- *The Color of Wealth: The Story Behind the U.S. Racial Wealth Divide* by Meizhu Lui, Barbara Robles, Betsy Leondar-Wright, Rose Brewer, Rebecca Adamson and United for a Fair Economy
- *Dear White Christians: For Those Still Longing for Reconciliation* by Jennifer Harvey
- *The Debt: What America Owes to Blacks* by Randall Robinson
- *Should America Pay?: Slavery and the Raging Debate on Reparations* by Raymond Winbush
- *Reparations, Yes! The Legal and Political Reasons Why New Afrikans, Black People in North America, Should Be Paid Now for the Enslavement of Our Ancestors* by Chokwe Lumumba
- *Where We Stand: Class Matters* by bell hooks

Legislation:
- H.R.40—Commission to Study and Develop Reparation Proposals for African-Americans Act: https://bit.ly/3y59Dlt

Manuals:
- Reparations Now Toolkit by Movement 4 Black Lives: https://bit.ly/3w3uAfi
- Reparations: The Time is Now! by Coming to the Table: https://bit.ly/2TbcURD

Organizations:
- Soul Fire Farm: https://www.soulfirefarm.org/
- Agricultural Reparations Map: https://bit.ly/3y0qlCq
- Coming to the Table: https://comingtothetable.org/
- Reparations Working Group: http://comingtothetable.org/reparations-working-group/
- N'COBRA (National Coalition of Blacks for Reparations in America): http://www.ncobraonline.org/
- Sogorea Te Land Trust: https://sogoreate-landtrust.org/
- Movement 4 Black Lives: https://m4bl.org/
- Reparations Platform: https://m4bl.org/policy-platforms/reparations/
- United Nations High Commissioner on Human Rights: https://www.ohchr.org/
- Statement on Reparations: https://bit.ly/2UgskEk

Direct Action

Articles:
- "Strategic Questioning: An Approach to Creating Personal & Social Change" by Fran Peavey: https://bit.ly/3oE1oJv
- "Still Time to Step Up: Reflections on Marshall Ganz's Organizing Method" by the New Syndicalist: https://bit.ly/372Z2Q7

Books:
- *The Politics of Nonviolent Action* by Gene Sharp
- *Beautiful Trouble: A Toolbox for Revolution* by Dave Oswald Boyd & Andrew Mitchell

Handouts:
- Direct Action Roles Cheat Sheet by Ruckus Society: https://ruckus.org/know-your-role/
- Messaging Guidance from the Movement 4 Black Lives: https://bit.ly/3w6rLK8

Manuals:
- "Action Strategy: A How-to Guide" by The Ruckus Society: https://bit.ly/3u6TYQ9
- "Training Packet" by Sugar Shack Alliance: https://bit.ly/34eORDF

- "Direct Action Manual" by Earth First!: https://bit.ly/2USNvfR
- "Climate Resistance Handbook: Or, I Was Part of a Climate Action. Now What?" by Daniel Hunter: https://bit.ly/2UFKFdV
- "Handbook for Nonviolent Action" by the War Resisters League: https://bit.ly/35YKtcn

Organizations:
- Beautiful Trouble: https://www.beautifultrouble.org/
- Global Nonviolent Action Database: https://nvdatabase.swarthmore.edu/
- Ruckus Society: https://ruckus.org/
- Albert Einstein Institution: https://www.aeinstein.org/
- James Lawson Institute: https://jameslawsoninstitute.org/

Videos:
- "The Power of Civil Disobedience" by Tim DeChristopher: https://bit.ly/3LRsFCV

Fierce Vulnerability and Integral Nonviolence

Articles:
- "Revolutionary Suicide: Risking Everything to Transform Society and Live Fully" by Lynice Pinkard: https://bit.ly/3vt9bxV
- "You Can't Kill the Spirit: Women and Nonviolent Action" by Pam McAllister: https://bit.ly/3lI4SdL
- "Hey Climate Movement! Deal with Personal Trauma" by Kritee (Kanko): https://bit.ly/2UYhkfb
- "The Revolution Will Be Titrated" by Tada Hozumi: https://bit.ly/3w5WKGw
- "Is There a Nonviolent Path to a Livable Future: A Conversation with Chris Moore-Backman" by Miki Kashtan: https://bit.ly/3w6XVFD
- "Fighting Injustice Can Cause Trauma" by Kazu Haga: https://bit.ly/3h6VFK2
- "We Need to Build a Movement that Heals Our Nation's Traumas" by Kazu Haga: https://bit.ly/3yfkz05

Audio:
- "Body Scan Meditation" by Jon Kabat Zinn: https://bit.ly/3jvqQka
- "Metta (loving kindness) Meditation" by Kazu Haga: https://bit.ly/3jtOtcE

Books (on Nonviolence):
- *Love In Action* by Thich Nhat Hahn
- *Healing Resistance: A Radically Different Response to Harm* by Kazu Haga
- *The Gandhian Iceberg: A Nonviolent Manifesto for the Age of the Great Turning* by Chris Moore-Backman
- *Conflict is Not Abuse: Overstating Harm, Community Responsibility, and the Duty of Repair* by Sarah Schulman
- *Nonviolent Communication: A Language of Life* by Marshall Rosenberg
- *The Power of Nonviolence* by Richard Gregg
- *Jesus and Nonviolence: A Third Way* by Walter Wink
- *Satyagraha and the Inner Life* by Clark Hanjian
- *The Search for a Nonviolent Future: A Promise of Peace for Ourselves, Our Families, and Our World* by Michael Nagler
- *Conflict is Not Abuse: Overstating Harm, Community Responsibility, and the Duty of Repair* by Sarah Schulman

Books (on Trauma Healing):
- *The Body Keeps The Score: Brain, Mind and Body in the Healing of Trauma* by Bessel Van der Kolk
- *Healing Collective Trauma: A Process for Integrating Our Intergenerational and Cultural Wounds* by Thomas Hübl
- *Building Resilience to Trauma: The Trauma and Community Resiliency Models* by Elaine Miller-Karas
- *A Complete Guide to Shadow Work*, by Scott Jeffrey
- *Healing the Soul Wound: Trauma Informed Counseling for Indigenous Communities* by Eduardo Duran
- *Internal Family Systems Skills Training Manual: Trauma-Informed Treatment for Anxiety, Depression, PTSD & Substance Abuse* by Frank Anderson, Richard Schwartz, and Martha Sweezy
- *My Grandmother's Hands: Racialized Trauma and the Pathways to Mending Our Hearts and Bodies* by Resmaa Menakem
- *The Politics of Trauma: Somatics, Healing and Social Justice*, by Staci Haines

- *Your Resonant Self: Guided Meditations and Exercises to Engage Your Brain's Capacity for Healing* by Sarah Peyton

Handouts:
- Embodied Self-Connection Process, Cultural Catalyst Network: https://bit.ly/3yfkz05
- Emotional Regulation Tools, East Point Peace Academy: https://bit.ly/364iAzq

Videos:
- "The Intent of Civil Disobedience" by Tim DeChristopher: https://bit.ly/3r7ei5v
- "What is Internal Family Systems?" by Richard Schwartz: https://bit.ly/3qAbegs
- "The Power of Vulnerability" by Brene Brown (Ted Talk): https://bit.ly/3dxgsV1

Websites:
- Re-evaluation Counseling: http://reevaluationcounseling.org/
- Empathy Brain: http://empathybrain.com/
- The Work of Byron Katie: https://thework.com/

Emergence

Articles:
- "The Tyranny of Structurelessness" by Jo Freeman: https://bit.ly/3hhAKTI
- "Using Emergence to Take Social Innovations to Scale" by Margaret Wheatley: https://bit.ly/3w41agX

Books:
- *Emergent Strategy: Shaping Change, Changing Worlds* by adrienne maree brown
- *Sacred Instructions: Indigenous Wisdom for Living Spirit-Based Change* by Sherri Mitchell
- *Leadership and the New Science: Discovering Order in a Chaotic World* by Margaret Wheatley
- *A Simpler Way* by Margaret Wheatley

- *Coming Back to Life: Practices to Reconnect Our Lives, Our World* by Joanna Macy

Websites:
- Margaret J. Wheatley: https://www.margaretwheatley.com/
- Emergent Strategy Ideation Institute: https://alliedmedia.org/speaker-projects/emergent-strategy-ideation-institute
- Reinventing Organizations: https://www.reinventingorganizations.com/ & https://reinventingorganizationswiki.com/

Decision-Making and Information Flow

Articles:
- "Decision Making Systems: From Either/Or to Integration" by Miki Kashtan: https://bit.ly/3EAKtif
- "Information Flow Systems: From Control to Transparency" by Miki Kashtan: https://bit.ly/31wjXIB

Organizations:
- Sociocracy for All: https://www.sociocracyforall.org/

Resource Flow

Articles:
- "Visionary Functioning: Shifting Resource Flow Systems from Incentive to Willingness" by Miki Kashtan: https://bit.ly/3GiztXh

Audio:
- "Questioning Money audio calls with Miki Kashtan": https://bit.ly/366vMUq
- "Money Makes the World Go Around podcast": https://bit.ly/3qJgZZp

Books:
- *Sacred Economics: Money, Gift & Society in the Age of Transition* by Charles Eisenstein
- *Women and the Gift Economy: A Radically Different Worldview Is Possible* by Genevieve Vaughan

Organizations:
- Resource Generation: https://resourcegeneration.org/
- Class Action: https://classism.org/
- Activist Class Cultures Kit: http://www.activistclasscultures.org/
- Service Space: https://www.servicespace.org/

Videos:
- "Designing for Generosity" by Nipun Mehta: https://bit.ly/3hoWqwX
- "In the Gift Economy, the More you Give, the Richer You Are" by Charles Eisenstein: https://bit.ly/3675qln
- "Maternal Gift Economy Movement by Breaking Through": https://bit.ly/3yeP8mx

Webpages:
- Gift Economics by East Point Peace Academy: https://www.eastpointpeace.org/gifteconomics
- Gift Economics by East Bay Meditation Center: https://eastbaymeditation.org/resources/gifteconomics/

Feedback and Conflict Engagement

Articles:
- "Receiving and Giving Effective Feedback" by the University of Waterloo's Centre for Teaching Excellence: https://bit.ly/3w216yk
- "How to Get Better at Giving (and Receiving) Feedback" by Deborah Petersen: https://bit.ly/3w9Fcci
- "Feedback Without Criticism by Miki Kashtan": https://bit.ly/3w5ypjR
- "Feedback Flow Systems: From Performance to Learning" by Miki Kashtan: https://bit.ly/3rHHvVB
- "Conflict Engagement: From Consequences to Capacity" by Miki Kashtan: https://bit.ly/3py4fof

Books:
- From the Little Books of Justice & Peacebuilding Series:
  - *Little Book of Circle Processes*
  - *Little Book of Conflict Transformation*
  - *Dialogue for Difficult Subjects*
  - *Cool Tools for Hot Topics*
- *Conflict Is Not Abuse: Overstating Harm, Community Responsibility, and the Duty of Repair* by Sarah Schulman
- *Nonviolent Communication: A Language of Life* by Marshall Rosenberg
- *Say What You Mean: A Mindful Approach to Nonviolent Communication* by Oren Jay Sofer and Joseph Goldstein
- *Sitting in the Fire: Large Group Transformation Using Conflict and Diversity* by Arnold Mindell

Websites:
- Yes! World: https://www.yesworld.org/
- Way of Council: https://waysofcouncil.net/
- Nonviolent Communication
  - Center for Nonviolent Communication: https://www.cnvc.org/
  - People of Color for Nonviolent Communication: https://www.poc4nvc.org/
  - Nonviolent Leadership for Social Justice: http://nlsj.learnnvc.org/

Self-Organizing/Decentralization

Articles:
- "Organizational Systems Overview" by Miki Kashtan [describing the five organizational systems featured in this handbook]: https://bit.ly/3EvJcJt
- "What are Social Alchemy Pods" by Adam Brock: https://bit.ly/3h39YPY
- "The Cellular Church: How Rick Warren's Congregation Grew" by Malcolm Gladwell: https://bit.ly/3jwtgyW

Books:
- *Reinventing Organizations: A Guide to Creating Organizations Inspired by the Next Stage of Human Consciousness* by Frédéric Laloux

- *This is an Uprising: How Nonviolent Revolt Is Shaping the Twenty-First Century* by Mark and Paul Engler
- *Swarmwise: The Tactical Manual to Changing the World* by Rick Falkvinge
- *The Starfish and the Spider: The Unstoppable Power of Leaderless Organizations* by Ori Brafman and Rod A. Beckstrom

Videos:
- SWARM, an 8-part video series by the Ayni Institute: https://bit.ly/3dtPmhJ

Websites:
- Reinventing Organizations:
  https://www.reinventingorganizations.com/
  https://reinventingorganizationswiki.com/

Contact

The Fierce Vulnerability Network is a decentralized and deeply relational project. If you are
reading this handbook, chances are you are already
in touch with someone who is actively involved—and
chances are that person is in your local area. We
encourage you to reach out to that person with any
questions and feedback you may have.

In addition, you can visit thefvn.org to stay
updated on the status of the network's forthcoming
onboarding process, and to learn how you can get
involved. We look forward to connecting with you!

Acknowledgments

Inspired by the Momentum model of organizing, the first generation of FVN's "DNA builders" understood that their work would be anonymous. These original DNA builders sought to define the network's DNA and to then dissolve as a group, without claim to the label of "founders." The intention here was that the network's principles and practices should be centered, as opposed to the individuals who first described them.

Five years and several iterations of DNA-building teams later, our relationship with this initial intention has become more complex. While still committed to centering the network's DNA, some DNA builders have come to believe it is important to openly acknowledge the individuals whose immense amount of work has helped bring this handbook into the world. In addition, some DNA builders have also expressed that transparently describing our origins feels essential in order not to obscure the fact that up until now the majority of DNA builders have been white. From the beginning, the predominant whiteness of our group has set significant limits on how our work has been envisioned and carried through. We continue to wrestle with what this means, especially as a network committed to racial healing, and we remain committed to practicing transparency about this key aspect of our journey. For this reason we've decided to favor transparency over our original intention to remain anonymous.

Hence, our grateful acknowledgement of all those who have served as DNA builders for the network thus far:

Sarah Baker, Tom Benevento, Evi Brouillet, Moona Cancino, Irma Serrano Carballido, Thomas Clarke-Hazlett, Morgan Curtis, Tim DeChristopher, Shawn Gregory, Kazu Haga, Sunny Hamrick, Ethan Hughes, Kritee (Kanko), Max Kee, Cliff Kindy,

Joanna Laws Landis, Marla Marcum, Corey Maxa, Chris Moore-Backman, Tim Nafziger, Andrea Novotney, Jay O'Hara, Pancho Ramos, Anthony Rogers-Wright, Aimee Ryan, Emma Schoenberg, Tyler Sheaffer, Erin Senghas Kassis, Leonie Smith, Karl Steyaert, Rebecca Sutton, Dan Truesdale, Margaret Wenger, Sarah Wilcox-Hughes, and Dayna Yildirim.

At various points in the creation of this handbook, Emma Schoenberg, Marla Marcum, Erin Senghas Kassis, Chris Moore-Backman, and Kazu Haga played a major role as "managing editors" of the manuscript that eventually became this handbook. We offer our thanks to them, and also to Calendula and Rosie, who represented the network's youth as honorary advisors to the DNA builders.

Hundreds of other individuals and many groups have leaned in and joined the experimentation that has given shape to the network. The following does not represent a complete list, but we have tried here to recognize and express our appreciation for those who have been most involved along the way. We're sorry for any unintended omissions.

In the beginning, Katie Chandler, Brenna Cussen, Dori Stone, Rivera Sun, Cliff Kindy, and Earl Martin offered critical help with the visioning of what was to come.

Along the way, invaluable support and contributions were offered by Aravinda Ananda, Jimmy Betts, Laurence Cole, Stephanie Elliot, Elaine Enns, Justine Epstein, Sarah Herrera, Miki Kashtan, Victor Lee Lewis, Elliot Martin, Te Martin, Silvio Finley McIntosh, astrid montuclard, Justin Novotney, Okogyeamon, Sierra Pickett, Lynice Pinkard, Imtiaz Rangwala, Jessica Reznicek, Carlos Saavedra, Nirali Shah, and Daniel Yildirim.

Four organizations—Climate Disobedience Center, Possibility Alliance, East Point Peace Academy, and Cultural Catalyst Network—have played a particularly meaningful role in supporting the emergence and development of the network. We offer them our deep thanks. Our sincere appreciation also goes to Vine & Fig (New Community Project), Living Downstream, Evening Star Farm, Great Turning Catholic Worker Farm, Weaving Earth, Green Valley Farm, Canticle Farm, and the Oakland Peace Center, for their gracious support and hospitality.

Heartfelt gratitude to Rachel Rolseth for the beautiful art and layout that makes our network's zine so special, and for the equally beautiful cover and interior art featured in this publication.

And a deep bow to brontë velez for the blessing of their deeply wise and generous foreword.

Lastly, sincere thanks to J. K. Fowler and everyone at Nomadic Press for the powerful role they are playing in the world of publishing, and for welcoming FVN into the family.

Nomadic Press Emergency Fund

Nomadic Press Black Writers Fund

Right before Labor Day 2020 (and in response to the effects of COVID), Nomadic Press launched its Emergency Fund, a forever fund meant to support Nomadic Press-published writers who have no income, are unemployed, don't qualify for unemployment, have no healthcare, or are just generally in need of covering unexpected or impactful expenses.

Funds are first come, first serve, and are available as long as there is money in the account, and there is a dignity centered internal application that interested folks submit. Disbursements are made for any amount up to $300.

All donations made to this fund are kept in a separate account. The Nomadic Press Emergency Fund (NPEF) account and associated processes (like the application) are overseen by Nomadic Press authors and the group meets every month.

On Juneteenth (June 19) 2020, Nomadic Press launched the Nomadic Press Black Writers Fund (NPBWF), a forever fund that will be directly built into the fabric of our organization for as long as Nomadic Press exists and puts additional monies directly into the pockets of our Black writers at the end of each year.

Here is how it works:

$1 of each book sale goes into the fund.

At the end of each year, all Nomadic Press authors have the opportunity to voluntarily donate none, part, or all of their royalties to the fund.

Anyone from our larger communities can donate to the fund. This is where you come in!

At the end of the year, whatever monies are in the fund will be evenly distributed to all Black Nomadic Press authors that have been published by the date of disbursement (mid-to-late December).

The fund (and associated, separate bank account) has an oversight team comprised of four authors (Ayodele Nzinga, Daniel B. Summerhill, Dazié Grego-Sykes, and Odelia Younge) + Nomadic Press Executive Director J. K. Fowler.

Please consider supporting these funds. You can also more generally support Nomadic Press by donating to our general fund via nomadicpress.org/donate and by continuing to buy our books.

As always, thank you for your support!

Scan the QR code for more information and/or to donate.

You can also donate at nomadicpress.org/store.